THROUGH THE COUNTRY OF

The Comanche Indians

IN THE FALL OF THE YEAR

1845

The Journal of a U. S. Army Expedition led by

LIEUTENANT JAMES W. ABERT

of the Topographical Engineers

Artist extraordinary whose paintings of Indians

and Their Wild West illustrate this book

EDITED BY JOHN GALVIN

PUBLISHED BY JOHN HOWELL—*Books*
MCMLXX

Library of Congress Catalogue Card No. 77-123-368

Printed in the United States of America

5000 COPIES

DESIGNED AND PRINTED BY LAWTON AND ALFRED KENNEDY

SAN FRANCISCO

FOR OUR SONS
SEAN, MICHAEL, MARK

PREFACE

This is the second of two volumes exhibiting the talents of an important but hitherto little known recorder of life in the early American West—Lieutenant James W. Abert of the U.S. Topographical Engineers, soldier and artist.

Three years ago, in *Western America in 1846–1847*, it was my good fortune to present Abert's original diary of his second western journey, with illustrations from the sketchbook that was the companion-piece to what he wrote. In that book was a record of the Old West such as few in our generation were familiar with, and pictures that even fewer had seen or even heard of.

His career indicated that there must have been more sketches and paintings, as well as known or unknown writing, from his hand. The question was, did more still survive?

The present volume answers emphatically, Yes. And the pictures reproduced in it, added to those represented in *Western America*, claim for him a high place as a painter of the Western scene in the 1840's.

The finding of the Abert paintings and drawings of 1845 is a story of persistence and benign conjuncture. The search narrowed, at last, to two present members of the Abert family: Mrs. Hamilton Abert, widow of a grandson of James W., and Mrs. G. Roger Harvey, great-granddaughter of Charles, brother of James. Both very kindly allowed us to add their material to our Abert collection.

Mrs. Hamilton Abert had the sketchbook of the 1845 expedition, which included some forty watercolors and pencil sketches. Mrs. Harvey had a bound copy of Abert's reports, printed as Congressional Documents, which Abert had prepared for his father and mother. He had added color to the monotone lithographic illustrations and had inserted a dozen watercolor sketches relating to the journey of 1845.

On a blank page in the front of the book he had written: "This book is not to be loaned to anyone. It is not in my power to renew the first report. All the colored drawings of the 1st Report were not printed with the printed copy of that Report."

Mrs. Harvey has supplied the information that after the death of Abert's parents the book passed to their son Charles and remained in his household until the death of the last of his children. Then it passed into the family of Charles Abert's granddaughter, Mary Constantia (Abert) Cook, and to her daughter, Catharine (Cook) Harvey, in 1966.

When the travel diary of 1845 first appeared in print, as a Congressional Document, it was headed "Journal of Lieutenant J.W. Abert from Bent's Fort to St.Louis"—a description that has since become less than satisfactory because Abert made *two* journeys from Bent's Fort to St. Louis, this first one in 1845 and the second in the winter of 1846–47. On the second journey he followed the Santa Fe trail, the usual route; on the first, he went a very different way.

He had set out as a member of Frémont's third exploring expedition, which reached Bent's Fort on the 2nd of August, 1845. "It was desirable," as Frémont later recounted in his *Memoirs*, "to make a survey of the prairie region to the southward, embracing the Canadian and other rivers. I accordingly formed a detached party, in charge of which I placed Lieutenants Abert and Peck, Lieutenant Abert being in chief command.

"Including these officers, the command consisted of thirty-three men, and I had the good fortune to secure my friend Mr. Fitzpatrick for their guide. I had endeavored to obtain the services of an Indian who knew well the country, and was a man of great influence, especially among the Comanches, but no offer that I could make would induce him to go.

"It happened that the Fort was well provisioned, and from its supplies we were able to furnish the party with a good outfit. This consisted principally of coffee and sugar for two months, several boxes of macaroni, and a quantity of rice, together with four fanegas of Mexican flour. In addition they took with them eight steers brought up on the prairie and therefore easy to drive. They were furnished with four large circular tents, and as the face of the country which was covered by the projected survey was not much broken, four wagons were added for their outfit and camp equipage. This outfit may appear luxurious for the prairie, but provisions go fast where thirty healthy men taking just the right quantity of exercise are to be fed three times a day. . . .

"On the 14th the two officers came to take leave of me. It is well to say here that on the journey to Bent's Fort I had been much prepossessed in their favor. They had shown themselves well qualified for such an expedition which as of course was entirely new to them. In this journey they had given evidence of the prudence and good judgment which enabled them to carry through successfully the expedition entrusted to their care.

"The next day I sent Lieutenant Abert his instructions, which were to survey the Canadian from its source to its junction with the Arkansas, taking in his way the Purgatory River, and the heads of the Washita; and on the 18th he commenced his journey down the Arkansas."

Abert's map, reproduced in the present volume, shows the route of his party southward through Raton Pass and eastward so as to observe the course of the Canadian River through what is now Oklahoma to its confluence with the Arkansas. Thence Abert went by ordinary road northeastward through Missouri towns to St. Louis.

His official reports of journeys in the service of the Government were among the best of their kind. They not only gave reliable and varied information as wanted by Government, Army, and prospective emigrants. They recorded what it was like to be "out beyond the settlements," where the buffalo roamed and the Indians took scalps and other people's horses. "Indians and buffalo," as Frémont remarked, "were the poetry and life of the prairie." And everything was strange, under skies radiant or grey; strangest among the harsh forms and barbaric colors of mesa and cañon, further south, where rivers were called "Colorado" because they ran red.

Abert was twenty-two when he made his journey of 1845, and the sparkle of youth is in his report of it. "We were almost wild with excitement," he exclaims, when nothing at all has happened; it is only that the scene was so beautiful. He was young, and the world was new. A wooded ravine of the Raton was as if "formed by the goddess Flora." On the Canadian "an Indian, mounted, now appeared and, as he swept along the horizon, looked a very giant"—seen with yet a schoolboy's eyes; for isn't there an echo from Scott's *Marmion*: "The warriors on the turrets high, moving athwart the evening sky, seemed forms of giant height"? In the 1840's the Romantic influence was strong, and a young man of education was likely to draw upon mythology and Borderer's tales to deck out his prose. Moreover, Abert's interests were wide, as is indicated in his remark at being left behind sick at Bent's Fort in 1846, "harassed with the thoughts of having come thus far and having been stopped just as I was entering upon a field of interest to the soldier, the archeologist, the historian, and the naturalist."

A letter he wrote to his brother Charles, in 1843, preserved by Charles Abert's great-granddaughter, tells of his "delightful plan of reading: until dinner the natural sciences—after dinner history—and finish off with poetry." The lieutenant bolsters his description of a landscape with a quotation from *King Lear* (though it may seem a far cry from antique Britain to south-central Oklahoma); and of course he does not forget the bush and brier of *A Midsummer Night's Dream*. The natural sciences, too, must have claimed a good share of his reading time. In his reports of both his western journeys he obviously does his best to record what is set before him from any of the natural kingdoms, animal, vegetable, or mineral. In the present report, moreover, he cites or at least mentions works by Cuvier, Audubon, Pennant the historian of quadrupeds, Murray the geographer, Dr. Harlan, Bernardin de Saint-Pierre, and the ornithologist and very minor poet Alexander Wilson. It may be remarked that he shared with Wilson the hackneyism "weltered in his gore," but Abert at least used it of an antelope; the bird man's victim was a flycatcher. Abert's hackneyed phrases are few: "the wily savage" and "sprung from his lair" are about the only ones noticeable. He is of his time in using "ever and anon" and "'twas but a moment."

If the original pencilled manuscript diary of this journey should come to light, presumably it would be found no less careless or uncertain in spelling, punctuation, and syntax than the manuscript diary of his journey of 1846–47. The copy available of the 1845 diary, made by a Government clerk or clerks, is smooth enough; most of its spellings accord with today's, though it often gives in two words or hyphenated a term that is now commonly closed up, and its punctuation generally accords with the sense though more commas are used than one would now prefer.

A few slips in spelling may be remarked: "dosing" for "dozing," "hair bell" for "harebell," "kill-dear" for "killdeer," "mains" for "manes," "red grass" for "reed grass," "roots" for "roosts." In the present volume these are silently corrected. A few spellings that are commoner to English than to American usage are retained, since they do not affect the sense. A few proper names are given as presumably Abert gave them, wrongly, but with due correction indicated. And a few words are supplied, enclosed in the customary square brackets, to carry the reader along with the least fuss.

For present purposes the diary is arbitrarily subdivided into numbered sections with headings and is paragraphed more freely than before. Since the engravings illustrating it as a Congressional Document do less than justice to Abert's sketches upon which they were based, they are omitted except the "sketch of a day's march" and the view of Antelope Buttes.

The manuscript copy preserved in the National Archives carries a mention of "President's Book No. 4." The President was James K. Polk. Western expansion was in the air, though it meant conflict with Mexico. Would there be conflict with Indians too? In 1845 three expeditions were sent out that were related to these matters: Kearny with dragoons made a long loop to South Pass—in southeastern Wyoming of today—and back to Fort Leavenworth; as he was returning, Frémont with an exploring party passed him, heading west to the Rocky Mountains and the region beyond; and from Bent's Fort, in what is now southeastern Colorado, Frémont sent a detachment under Lieut. Abert south and eastward along the Canadian River to its confluence with the Arkansas, not far from the western border of Arkansas state, a distance of some six hundred miles through wild country where Indians were hazards. For some days and nights, these white men were aware that Indians in large numbers were moving parallel with them and never far away. It is an unexpected and extraordinary scene in Abert's account when a friendly Indian who has elected to travel with the expedition makes a long speech in a loud voice to an unseen audience. He is telling the Indians that the white men are not Texans (with whom the Comanches were long in bitter conflict), but Americans. Abert's party continues on the alert against possible attack, but no attack comes.

Danger of sudden and violent death is not entirely removed, however. In the last stage of the journey the two lieutenants and one of their men go ahead of the party, only to learn that they have unknowingly risked being shot on sight by Cherokee Indian settlers for three of the desperadoes known as the "Starr boys." Travel-worn, sunburnt and unshaven, and dressed in frontier fashion, they didn't look, just then, like spruce exemplars of the American military.

Lieut. William G. Peck, the second in command, was of the same age as Abert though of a later West Point class. For guide and counselor there was Thomas Fitzpatrick, known to Indians as Broken Hand; he had just returned from South Pass with Kearny's dragoons, and Kearny praised him as "an excellent woodsman." Also to go with Abert's party as far as Bent's trading post on the Canadian were "a good hunter," John Hatcher, and another, Caleb Greenwood. Thirty men and two servants filled out the roster, with sixty or so horses and mules, and four wagons.

The wagons were to be a subject of remarks. A pack train might have made the journey with less difficulty. The diarist of Col. Dodge's expedition of 1834 had remarked soon after the troopers were on their way that wagons were "a great drawback to military expeditions." Abert came to the same conclusion. Indian trails, he wrote, are "always the most practicable routes through the country; but as they had no wagons to encumber them, we were sometimes led into difficulties which required the constant exercise of our ingenuity to overcome." And later: "This morning we had a serious debate as to the expediency of taking our wagons further or abandoning them to the Indians. They are a source of continued delay and vexation." But he got them through; "Nothing is impossible," he said, "if man will only clap his shoulder to the wheel." It was the first time that wagons had gone all the way from Bent's Fort to Fort Gibson.

The region was not unknown. Voyageurs from French Canada were there early; in the summer of 1740 the Mallet brothers, with their half-dozen companions, were on the Canadian in canoes, which they made from elm bark. In 1820, Maj. Stephen Long and his exploring party passed through. Washington Irving, making his "tour on the prairie," crossed the North Fork of the Canadian in 1832. In 1834, Col. Dodge with a force of dragoons went out the Canadian from Fort Gibson to an Indian council. And in 1843, Capt. Nathan Boone, youngest son of the well-known Daniel, led an expedition yet further from Fort Gibson, up across the Cimarron to the Santa Fe trail and back again.

Records of all these and other journeys are available. So are some noteworthy records by artists: Titian Peale and Samuel Seymour, of Philadelphia, whose surviving works include some of the earliest portraits of Indians in the West, were with Maj. Long in 1820. Catlin, with Col. Dodge in 1824, sketched at Fort Gibson some of his best works, including the portrait of the Wichita girl, captured by the Osages, whom the dragoons were returning to her own people. The Creeks on the North Fork of the Canadian, whom Capt. Boone visited, were subjects of sketches by John Mix Stanley.

As a recorder with pencil, brush, and colors Abert is a worthy member of this valuable company. He was a ready and accurate draughtsman and had a quick eye for color. He put on paper what he saw, faithfully and with vitality, and at times charmingly. His father, Col. John James Abert, longtime head of the Topographical Bureau, had a hand for mapmaking; perhaps his work attracted the attention and interest of the beginner at home. Draughtsmanship was taught at West Point, where Abert was a cadet. And one of Col. Abert's close friends, William G. Williams, an officer of engineers who was to lose his life in the War with Mexico, was a practicing artist, some of whose portraits are mentioned in the exhibition record of the National Academy of Design for the early 1840's. Did he, too, attract the young man to an artist's endeavors?

As a writer of travel diaries Abert did what the best travel writers have always done: he carried his reader with him. He still does. And his watercolor drawings intensify the vitality of his narratives. We are all in his debt for his records of the region as it looked to a high-spirited, alert, and responsible young commander of an expedition "on the Upper Arkansas and through the country of the Comanche Indians in the fall of the year 1845."

Bents Fort Aug 2ⁿ Sat.

ACKNOWLEDGMENTS

I should like to express my thanks to the National Archives of the United States for providing a microfilm of Lieutenant Abert's report of his travels in 1845 as written out by a Government copyist. In the absence of the original handwritten diary, the whereabouts of which is not known to me, the film has supplied a contemporary manuscript against which to check the printed version of Abert's report as a Congressional Document. I have used also Abert's printed reports as given by him to his parents with some marginal jottings by his own hand.

    Harold A. Small's great interest and Warren Howell's enthusiasm made it possible for me to secure the watercolors that illustrate this book; for this achievement and for their skills which add to this work I give them my thanks. Dr. Woodrow Borah's many kindnesses and practical help are acknowledged with appreciation.   J.G.

TABLE OF CONTENTS

MAPS

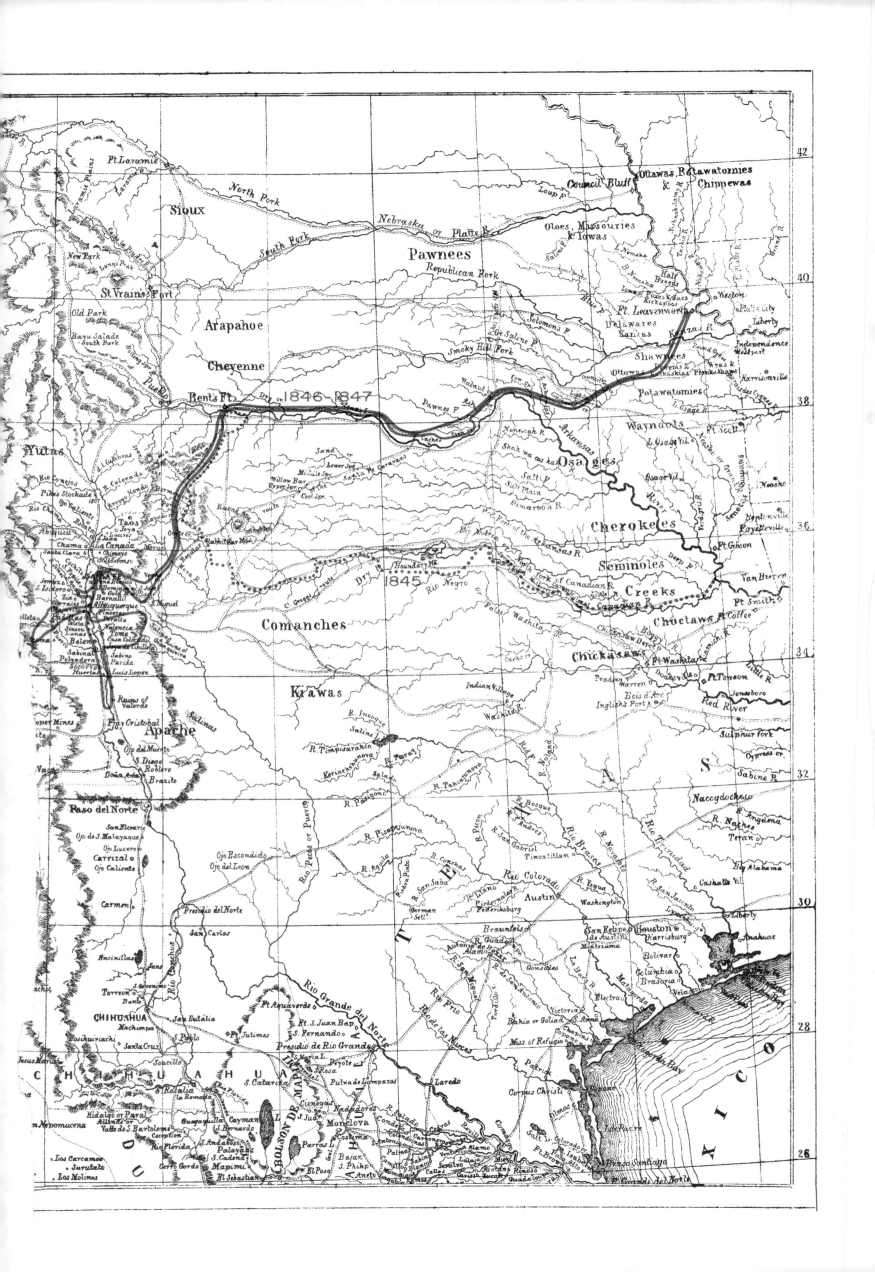

MAP
OF
MEXICO
&
CALIFORNIA

Compiled from the latest authorities

BY

JULS HUTAWA

Lith! Second St. 45 St. Louis, Mo.

.2ᵈ EDITION

(Center Section)

LIST OF ILLUSTRATIONS

BIOGRAPHIES IN BRIEF

Abert, James William. Born in Mount Holly, N.J., November 18, 1820; graduated from Princeton in 1838, the year in which his father, John James Abert, became colonel commanding the Corps of Topographical Engineers, U.S. Army; graduated from the U.S. Military Academy, 1842; brevet 2nd lieut. 5th Infantry, July 1, 1842, and with that regiment in garrison at Detroit a year; transferred to Topographical Engineers May 24, 1843; assistant topographical engineer in survey of the northern lakes, 1843–1844; with Frémont's third exploring expedition and detached in command of an expedition down the Canadian River, 1845; 2nd lieut., May 27, 1846; with Kearny's "Army of the West" and in New Mexico engaged in a survey of that new American possession, 1846 (when there awaited him home from campaign his young wife Jane, née Stone, and infant son William); taught drawing at West Point two years; 1st lieut., March 3, 1853; captain, July 1, 1856; served two years in Florida; in 1860 traveled in Europe studying military affairs and visiting arsenals and forts; returned to participate in the Civil War and served in the Valley of the Shenandoah from June, 1861, to September, 1862; major, Corps of Engineers, March 3, 1863; resigned, out of health, and brevetted lieutenant-colonel, June 25, 1864; reinstated, and retired January 14, 1895; died at Newport, Kentucky, August 10, 1897, survived by the wife of his second marriage, Lucy (née Taylor), and several children.

Peck, William Guy. Born in Litchfield, Conn., October 16, 1820; graduated from the U.S. Military Academy, first in his class, a distinction he had held throughout the four years' course, 1844; brevet 2nd lieut. Topographical Engineers, July 1, 1844; with Abert's expedition down the Canadian River, 1845; with Abert making a survey of New Mexico, 1846; taught mathematics at West Point from 1847 to 1855; 2nd lieut., May 31, 1848; 1st lieut., March 3, 1853; resigned October 20, 1855; professor of physics and civil engineering at the University of Michigan to 1857; professor of mathematics at Columbia College from 1857 until his death in 1892; assisted his father-in-law, Professor Charles Davies, in compiling a *Dictionary of the Mathematical Sciences*, published in New York in 1855; author of school and college textbooks in mathematics; died February 7, 1892, at Greenwich, Conn.

1. Start of the Journey · Bent's Fort · Cheyennes and Delawares

Bent's Fort on the Arkansas River,
Saturday, August 9th, 1845.

In compliance with orders from Capt. Frémont, I this day moved across the river, to take command of the party detached for the survey of Purgatory Creek, the waters of the Canadian and False Washita.

My duties in charge of a separate command commenced at the trading establishment of Bent's Fort, upon the upper waters of the Arkansas. Until our arrival there the whole party was under the command of Capt. Frémont, who will no doubt detail all that was worthy of note up to that time; my narrative, therefore, will be confined to the events of my command after leaving Bent's Fort and until our return to St. Louis.

Before entering upon the daily account which always forms the complement of a military reconnoissance I deem it necessary to give some description of Bent's Fort, as it constitutes our point of departure and shows the character of the military structures which experience has decided to be best adapted to the country. It was to us the most interesting point of our trip, as it gave a fine opportunity of seeing what we called "wild Indians" in contradistinction to those who dwell in the vicinage of the settlements. We arrived at Bent's Fort, or Fort William, on the 2d of August, and found that Col. Kearney with his dragoons had passed us—a cause of great regret, as we could have procured from him many things which would have added to our comfort.

The fort is composed of a series of rooms resembling casemates and forming a hollow square, the entrance on the east side. A round tower on the left as you enter and another diagonally opposite constitute the flanking arrangements. The outer walls, which are nearly two feet in thickness, intersect in the axes of the towers, thus permitting their faces to be completely enfiladed; the outside walls of the enceinte and towers, pierced with loopholes, are continued four feet above the flat roofs which serve for the banquette, which being composed of clay cannot be fired by inflammable substances that might be cast upon it; the whole is built of "adobes," sun-burnt brick, formed of clay and cut straw, in size about four times as large as our common bricks. The roofs are sustained by poles. On the west side is the cattle yard, which is surrounded by a wall so high as effectually to shelter them. The coping of the wall is planted with cacti which bear red and white flowers. Scattered around the fort in different cages we saw some of the birds of this region—the mockingbird, Turdus polyglottus, magpie, Corvus pica, and two of the bald-headed eagle, Falco leucocephalus.

I endeavoured to obtain information with reference to our southern route; but the only person who knew much of the country through which we should have to pass was a Kioway Indian, called in his own language "Tah-kai-buhl," a man of great influence among all the Indians in that region, particularly with the Comanches, who were greatly to be feared. Capt. Frémont made him most tempting offers to undertake the guidance of our party through these hostile Indians, but he refused to go with us.

The cañons on the Purgatory and Canadian were represented as impassable. I had four wagons in [my] charge and found that preparing a party at the foot of the Rocky Mountains to undertake an arduous and dangerous journey was much more difficult than if we had started from the settlements.

On the 7th of August a large party of the Cheyenne Indians came dashing up to the Fort. They were all, both men and women, mounted astride of their horses, and came galloping up abreast, singing a song of triumph in honor of the success of a war party which had just returned with a Pawnee scalp. Their song was accompanied by the music of four tambourines, and all the sounds seemed jerked out by the motion of the horses, which galloped in perfect time. They then collected around the Fort, and we had a fine opportunity of observing them. The successful warrior and his relatives were covered with black paint; he was called Little Crow, or "Oco-chee-tah-nahun."

In the afternoon I was kindly invited by the gentlemen of the Fort to see a scalp dance. On going up I found about forty women with faces painted red and black, nearly all cloaked with Navaho blankets and ornamented with necklaces and earrings, dancing to the sound of their own voices and the four tambourines, which were beat upon by the men. I was informed that the songs were in honor of those who had distinguished themselves, holding them up for imitation, and deriding one whose behaviour had called his courage in question. In dancing they made a succession of jumps in which the feet were raised but little from the ground. When they first commenced, they were placed shoulder to shoulder on different sides of a square; they then moved forwards towards the centre, raising a yell resembling the war whoop; they then dispersed and retook their stations in order to repeat the same movements; some had lances, some war clubs, whilst the mother of Little Crow had the honor of bearing the scalp. I never in my life saw a happier set. The women laughed and jumped in rapturous delight, whilst their husbands and lovers were grouped around on the roofs of the Fort looking on most complacently. Again the figure of the dance was changed; the dancers, placed in one continuous ring, move slowly round. I happened to be near the press for packing furs, in the centre of the square, and had a fine opportunity for taking sketches.

On the 8th the gentlemen at the Fort induced Yellow Wolf, "O-cum-who-wust," the head chief of the Shieene [Cheyenne] nation, to sit for me. After finishing the sketch, I showed him my book, when, seeing some of his tribe whose likenesses were colored, he evinced great dissatisfaction and said I had represented him badly; but we made him understand that the pencil sketch was incomplete, which seemed to satisfy him. We were much amused in the afternoon with a Sioux called "Shonka-mah-toh," the Dog Bear. I had made a sketch of his full face, when he insisted that some Pawnee scalp locks attached to his own should also be represented; to satisfy his vanity I was obliged to make a profile. This man belonged to a band called "Brulé." He had a fine eye for colors and aided me in selecting those I wished to use. His dress was quite elegant, consisting of a handsome buffalo robe ornamented with porcupine quills and tufts of red worsted, buckskin leggins with broad bands of beads on the outer seam, and [a] handsome bow with a quiver of panther skin filled with arrows, and the indispensable breechcloth. All the Indians pull out the beard and eyebrows with tweezers made of brass, tin, or a spiral wire, but they cultivate the hair of the head to a great length, particularly the scalp lock, which often trails on the ground, and is ornamented with large plates of silver.

In the evening I got a fine sketch of "Mis-stan-star," a Shieene [Cheyenne] squaw, who, although she has been married several years and has two children, yet shows signs of having been a remarkably handsome woman. Having a white man for her husband, she has not been obliged to work; therefore her hands are in all their native beauty, small, delicately formed, and with tapering fingers. Her wavy hair, unlike the Indians' generally, was fine and of silken softness. She put on her handsomest dress in order to sit for me. Her cape and undergarment were bordered with bands of beads, and her beautiful leggins, which extended only to the knee, were so nicely joined with the moccasin that the connection could not be perceived, and looked as neat as the stockings of our eastern belles; and the modest attitude in which she sits is characteristic, but will be best conceived by the sketch. I also made a sketch of her brother, "Nah-cot-se-west," whom I represented smoking, in compliance with the importunities of his mother; for those only are allowed to smoke who have done some valiant deed, which is termed in this country a "coup."

Whilst walking along the riverbank I observed a number of squaws and children bathing, and stopped to transfer them to my portfolio, but was immediately surrounded by men and women anxious to see my book; I gratified them, and they would laugh in high glee as they recognised each familiar face; but their greatest merriment burst forth upon beholding "Isse-wo-ne-mox-ist," a very old man who wore his hair twisted into an immense horn projecting from his forehead; his hair was of a reddish grey, which differs somewhat from our received notions of the color of the Indians' hair, but I have seen boys around Bent's Fort who could not have been more than 12 years of age whose hair was quite grey.

On Saturday, the 9th, Mr. Chabonard called for me to accompany him on a visit to "Nah-co-men-si," or the Winged Bear, more generally known as Old Bark. He is second in rank to Yellow Wolf and is remarkable for perseverance, enterprise, and bravery; although now very old, yet about a year since he went as far as the settlements on a war trail. He regretted much that he had not a robe for me emblazoned with the history of his bold achievements, but unfortunately he had given them all away.

His daughter is the belle of the nation, and although pressed by innumerable suitors, whose offerings to the amount of numbers of horses have frequently been tied to the door of her lodge, she will not relinquish her freedom. She is very rich, possessing several complete suits of buckskin, all most tastefully ornamented. She wears a singular girdle, the portion around the waist covered with scarlet cloth and the whole studded with large flat gilt buttons. She is called "Am-eer-tschee," the Fast Walker. Previous to sitting she covered her face with vermilion, drawing black streaks over it, as represented.

The women are remarkable for the neatness with which they arrange their hair: being parted across the middle of the head, it is drawn to the ear and formed into plaits which extend nearly to the waist; but it is never so long as that of the men.

About 12 o'clock we went to the Fort to attend a council to be held between the Delawares and Cheyennes. It appeared that 14 months previous to our arrival the Cheyennes and Sioux had massacred a party of 15 Delawares in this vicinity. Shortly after, meeting with Capt. Frémont, they desired him to bear pacific proposals to the Delawares, who, they feared greatly, would avenge this outrage; and their fears were not a little increased when they saw them now united with Capt. Frémont—for he had engaged several of them to accompany him across the mountains. Lieut. Peck and myself were amongst the few whites present. We were all seated on buffalo robes upon the ground, so ranged around the council chamber that our backs could be supported against the wall. Each party spoke in his own dialect, which was first translated into English, then into that of the other party.

The Delawares opened the council by a short address, concluding with the presentation of a curious pipe which they said had been smoked in an assemblage of twenty-seven different nations. Yellow Wolf carried round the pipe, and I observed each one had a peculiar form in receiving it, with all of which he seemed perfectly familiar. To one he offered it the stem downwards, to another with the bowl on the ground. Some offered a whiff to the Great Spirit, others to the points of the rising and setting sun, and each had some peculiar "medicine," or mystery, which must be strictly observed.

A white, familiarly known as Bill Garey, acted as Cheyenne interpreter. A long residence amongst them had enabled him to repeat all their graceful and expressive gestures, which add the poetry of motion to the music of their language, of which gestures form an important part. Yellow Wolf said a few words, after which Old Bark spoke as follows:

"We have been in great dread lest you should make war upon us, and, although our women and children have been suffering for food, were afraid to venture forth, for we are now weak and poor, and our ground diminished to a small circle. The whites have been amongst us and destroyed our buffalo, antelope, and deer and have cut down our timber; but we are so desirous to keep peaceful that we take no notice of it, for we regard the Delawares and whites as one people.

"My heart is now exceeding glad, and we feel as if the whole sky had been lifted up to a great height. I never wished to see the prairie deluged with blood, and was glad when I beheld this pipe, which I shall always reverence as great medicine. It shall be handed down to our children as a memorial of this day, when we re-established our firm friendship with our brothers towards the rising sun. I have at my village a fine horse which I will give you."

The Delawares then invited them to a grand council to be held at the Salt Plains, when all the neighbouring nations would be present and should ratify this treaty of peace and unite against those who would not enter into the combination. One of the gentlemen of the Fort then addressed them, censuring them severely for their misconduct. He said that although the whites and Delawares bear being killed a long time, and did not revenge every outrage, yet they had their eyes and ears open, and the Great Father [President Polk] had already sent Col. Kearney on a war trail through the country to call all offenders to account; that he had met with the Sioux and had great difficulty in preventing his braves from "rubbing them out" entirely. We then dispersed.

The speeches made on the occasion were written out in full from the mouth of the interpreter, but are too long for insertion in this place. All the speakers kept their seats whilst addressing the assembly. The meeting was conducted throughout with great decorum.

In the afternoon I had an opportunity of seeing the men dance, when a young brave went through the ceremony of counting his "coups." He was mounted on a piebald horse mysteriously marked with red clay; he would ride up to the drummers and relate his exploits, and it was their duty to tap the drums when they knew his narrations to be true. After finishing his rodomontades he rode off a few steps whilst the rest joined in a dance, giving the hero time to recall some other exploit. Old Bark, who was one of the spectators, pointed out his son, who also made himself an object of attraction by his extravagant contortions. He desired me to sketch him. Many of the dancers had rattles, some lances with curved handles, and not a few had fans to protect their complexions.

On the evening of the 9th, Lieut. Peck and myself crossed the river in order to organize our camp, which was placed about one-fourth of a mile east of Bent's Fort. We had great reason to congratulate ourselves on the exchange of our cook—quite an important personage on the prairie, for on his economy and skill the comfort of the party greatly depends. Today we were a little annoyed by Indians who came prowling around in order to take advantage of our unarranged camp. In the night I was aroused by a noise and on going out found a half-starved dog; as I drew up my rifle the poor creature came and cringed at my feet, whining piteously, so I gave him his life, and suppose we lost a few pieces of meat which were lying on the scaffolds over the fire.

The next morning I went out to pay Capt. Frémont a visit. Mr. Kern, the artist who accompanies his expedition, showed some sketches by Old Bark's son, in which he had represented himself killing some Pawnees with the lance. The execution was quite good and exhibited considerable feeling for design and proportion.

On the 12th, Mr. Fitzpatrick joined me and we immediately proceeded to take up our line of march, which enabled us to obtain a position affording finer grazing for our animals. I was at once delighted with the carefulness of our guide. He directed one to loosen the noose which, passing round the mules' nose and neck, held them so closely together as to prevent their eating; another, never to tie his mules in the bushes, for alarmed at every rustle they are constantly looking wildly around expecting some enemy. These things may appear trifling, but those who have been upon the prairie know well how much depends upon the care and attention bestowed upon the animals.

On the 13th, we made a second move in order to get a new grazing ground. Some of the men amused themselves with fishing but were not very successful; a few catfish were the only specimens of the piscatory genus that these turbid waters afford. The banks were overgrown with tall reeds which resemble the canebrakes of Arkansas. I went out on a hunt, but my mule was restive and on the starting of a deer she became so unmanageable as completely to baffle all attempts to aim my gun.

The next morning (14th) we made our farewell visit to Capt. Frémont's camp. It was all in the bustle of preparation for a long and toilsome journey. Capt. Frémont regretted much that he had not obtained the howitzer,[1] which, unfortunately, did not reach Westport until we had left. He thought it would be of great service, particularly as we had no one who understood the Comanche language. Indeed, we all expected an encounter with these Indians, through whose country we would be obliged to pass, and our exposure would be prolonged by the slowness with which we would be constrained to move with our wagons along the deeply cañoned rivers. Recent difficulties with the Texans,[2] in which the Comanches had suffered the loss of forty of their bravest men and chiefs, had so incensed them that matters appeared quite serious. It was hoped, however, that many of them would be assembled with the Kioways at Bent's trading houses on the Canadian, and we would have with us Mr. Hatcher, who had great influence with the Kioways, having traded with them at that place.

The picturesque costume of the people around causes involuntary pleasure to one accustomed to the stiff dress of the American citizen. Here there was the greatest diversity, but that of the old voyageur seems to merit our attention. He is dressed in buckskin breeches with deep fringe along the outer seam, a leather strap across the shoulders to which is affixed the awl and bullet mould and sustaining the powder horn and bullet pouch, which also contains some caps and the indispensable flint and steel. Each wears some gaudy-colored calico shirt and a belt bearing the scalping knife. The unerring rifle, with its cover and wiping stick, a blanket overcoat, together with a couple of red, blue, or white blankets, constitute his whole equipment when mounted on his untiring mule.

Our command consisted of the following persons:

Pierre Balanger	John Carroll
William Bowers	Isaac Cooper
Patrick Bradley	Stephen Cooper

---

1. On his preceding western expedition Frémont took along a howitzer until it could be taken no further, and abandoned it in the Sierra snows. "It had commanded respect for us," he wrote, "on some critical occasions." See, in his *Report*, his travel-diary entry for January 29, 1844.

2. The "Council House fight." Comanches who had come to San Antonio to demand ransom for white captives were themselves seized when assembled in the courthouse, and resisted, with consequent bloodshed. See Bancroft, *History of the North Mexican States and Texas* (1889), Vol. II, pp. 324–325.

Oliver Dewey	Charles Marand
Walter Harding	Edward Morin
John Harper	Edmund Philebert
Lester Hulin	Narcisse Pichée
Loven [Loren] Jeffers	Joseph Rivarre
Thomas Jemison	Solomon Rivarre
Howell Jonvier	Zephyr Rochon
François Latulippe	Edward Russel
Duncan Linn	Paul Vachard
Joseph Linn	John Wainwright
John McKee	Joseph Yount

Also, Raphael Harrison and Silas Sublette, two colored men.

Mr. Hatcher and Mr. Greenwood accompanied me only as far as Bent's houses. These, with Lieut. Peck, Mr. Fitzpatrick, and myself, formed our complement.

Our company was divided into four messes, each mess furnished with a circular tent capable of sheltering 8 or 10 persons, and amongst them were distributed the 4 wagons, also the 56 mules and 7 horses which had been provided for the party. We were better supplied with the necessaries of life than on the outward trip. We endeavoured to economize by making a new dish in imitation of the Spanish "atole," which was ever after a standing joke on the proposer. Now, through the agency of Messrs. Bent and St. Vrain, we had procured eight fanegas[3] of unbolted Mexican flour, also plenty of coffee, and as much sugar as, with economy, would last us for two months; three or four boxes of maccaroni and a small quantity of rice were added as luxuries; so that, with eight prairie-fed beeves which we drove along, to use on the emergency of not finding game, we considered ourselves pretty well supplied. We were not so fortunate, however, in a supply of instruments, having but a single sextant and [a] chronometer for the determination of our latitudes and longitudes—a circumstance that involved us in continual anxiety for their safety. The stock of meteorological instruments brought out by Capt. Frémont had been reduced so low by repeated accidents that he was unable to furnish us with even a single barometer. And as we afterwards passed through regions of deep interest to the naturalist, we often regretted the deficiencies in the original outfit which deprived us of the means of making suitable collections of the fauna, avia, flora, et cetera; but, the matter being irremediable in that country, our regrets were useless.

The delays of the last few days will be of lasting service to our animals in giving them needful rest before recommencing a long and toilsome journey, and in enabling the party to make all necessary arrangements.

2. THE ROUTE · UP THE PURGATORY · APACHES · PRAIRIE DOGS · A MUSTANG

Friday, August 15th.—Camp No. 2. Agreeably to the orders of Capt. Frémont, this day received, we prepared to make a survey of the Canadian from its source to its junction with the Arkansas,[4] taking in our route the Purgatory and the heads of the Washita, called by the Indians Buffalo Creek and Cut-nose Creek. As before observed, Mr. Tho. Fitzpatrick was to be our guide; a gentleman eminently qualified in every respect to fill the arduous and responsible station assigned him. Having spent many of the best years of his life exposed to the toils and vicissitudes of the mountain and the prairie, he had acquired an intimate knowledge of the Indian character, which enabled

---

3. Frémont in his *Memoirs* (1887), p. 426, says "four fanegas." A Mexican *fanega* was equivalent to about two bushels; see Wislizenus, *Memoir* (1848), p. 141.

4. Here, Abert's interest in place names appears in his only footnote: "This word is usually written Arkansas, but in an old map, 1775, I find it written 'Akansas, the fair men.'"

him to conduct our little party safely and successfully through a country inhabited by numerous and powerful hordes of people long notorious for their faithlessness and treachery. He had accompanied Capt. Frémont and rendered signal services in the long and arduous campaigns of 1843 and 1844, in Oregon and Upper California, and was now just returning from the South Pass,[5] where he had guided the dragoons under the command of Col. Kearney on one of the most rapid and successful expeditions ever made on the western prairies. The preservation of our party was due to his vigilance and discretion.

Saturday, 16th.—All our preparations being completed, we began to descend the Arkansas, having bid adieu to the gentlemanly proprietors of Fort William. Our route lay along the right bank of the river, one continued series of hills and sand plains. We noticed a profusion of prairie sage, Artemisia tridentata, being about the only shrub that grows in these sandy regions. This plant seems to love a dry and arid soil, covering, as it does, millions of acres of the great desert at the eastern base of the Rocky Mountains. In some places it grew so luxuriantly that the stalks might be used for fuel. We were disappointed in not seeing even one specimen of the sage cock, Tetrao urophasianus, which is so extravagantly fond of feeding on this plant that its flesh becomes so embittered as to render it perfectly uneatable. Notwithstanding the abundance of the plant, we did not see a single specimen of this bird during the trip. Cacti were numerous, and a species of Cucurbitaceæ, Cucurbita aurantia, bearing a small spherical gourd, orange-colored. These plants are characteristic of the dry sandy plains. As we moved along, some deer sprang from the dead tangled wildwood of the Arkansas bottom, and antelopes dashed across the prairie, much to our astonishment, for we supposed they had become almost extinct in the vicinity of the Fort. One of the men killed a fine fat doe, which furnished us with a grateful meal after [our] having lived so many days on tough beef.

About noon we arrived at the junction of the Purgatory, or Las Animas,[6] with the Arkansas, and found a beautiful camping ground under a grove of large cottonwood trees. Although early in the day, we concluded to stop in order to determine our position. Our latitude was found to be 38° 06′ 00″. The latitudes and longitudes which we obtained are not laid down as absolute; the determination of longitude, being dependant upon the chronometer, must necessarily be imperfect. Although the chronometer might be accurately rated on setting out, it is hardly to be supposed that a transportation of more than a thousand miles, over the rough country we were obliged to pass, would not have occasioned some slight irregularity. As we started from a point the position of which had been determined with considerable accuracy, and arrived at one very well known, we were enabled so to account for the irregularities of the chronometer as to give very good proximate results. The latitudes are more independent of the chronometer and consequently entitled to be considered more accurate. The slight errors both of latitude and longitude we have endeavoured to overcome, as far as the nature of them would permit, by numerous and repeated observations.

The Purgatory was here 20 yards wide, with a rapid current like all the rivers near mountains. It is highly charged with sedimentary matter, averaged 2 feet in depth; banks steep, and its surface now 8 feet below the level of the prairie; being well wooded, its course is distinctly traceable for a long distance. We already find that the provisions are going with astonishing rapidity, and conclude to give every mess its share. An equal partition was therefore made to the four messes which composed the command, and they were warned of the consequences of waste in a land where one

5. South Pass, in what is now western Wyoming, provided a way through the Rocky Mountains and gave access to trails leading to the Oregon country and to northern and central California. Since that route offered water, grazing for animals, game for hunters, and a not too difficult road, it was preferred by early travelers to the southern route westward from the valley of the Rio Grande by way of the Gila River and the Mojave Desert.

6. The Purgatory was also called by its French name the Purgatoire—corrupted to "Picketwire"—and by its Spanish names Las Animas and, like a number of other streams in that region, the Colorado.

cannot even rely upon finding buffaloes. At night Lieut. Peck and myself walked around the camp to caution the guard, for a couple of Indians, completely enrolled in their blankets, were dozing near one of the campfires, and perhaps might be tempted to purloin some of our equipments. This stream affords fine wintering ground for the Indians, on account of the abundance of deer that are found along its banks. We were astonished at seeing great numbers of fallen trees, but afterwards learned that the Indians are in the habit of foraging their horses in winter on the tender bark and young twigs of the cottonwood, which offered a satisfactory explanation.

Sunday, August 17th.—At 6 o'clock we struck our tents and left Camp No. 3, moving in a southwesterly direction up the Purgatory. For a distance of 6 or 8 miles we had the same sandy traveling as yesterday, when we reached a more broken country, the high bluffs occasionally sending a spur to the very water's edge. These cliffs form the boundary of what remains of the tableland through which the Purgatory and other streams have excavated their deep valleys. The rocks over which we passed are of soft brown sandstone, easily eroded by the action of waters. The rocky strata are nearly horizontal and highly ferruginous. One rock of considerable extent presented the curious appearance of a mosaic pavement, being cut into regular forms by seams of iron, which, from their great capability of resisting the action of the atmosphere, stood out in high relief. As we turned a point of the tableland we again caught sight of the Rocky Mountains; at the first view they appeared like a line of faint blue clouds lying close along the horizon. To the southwest the "Wah-To-Yah," or Spanish Peaks,[7] raised their twinned heads, forming a limit in that direction to the visible range, whilst to the northwest the snowy summit of Pike's Peak was faintly discernible.

We met a party of Apache Indians at this place. The women and children were in the train with the mules and dogs; some were riding in their fashionable gigs [travois], which are formed of the lodge poles, the largest extremities of which are allowed to trail on the ground; the other ends, crossed on the mule's or dog's back, form shafts upon which a basket is affixed to contain the women, children, and chattels. The men, on their prancing steeds, were dashing about in search of fruit and game.

One of them stopped to make a confession which certainly does credit to Indian honesty. He said "that for the last few days they had been searching for game but could not find any; that his squaws and children were crying for meat and he had not a morsel to give them; the extremity of their sufferings had that morning urged him to kill an ox which he met on the road, and he wished us to intercede with the people at the Fort. Urgent necessity had obliged him to do wrong; but he intended to pay for it, and should retain the tail, which he showed us, as a remembrance of his indebtedness." Mr. Fitzpatrick told him he had done perfectly right; that the white people would not be angry if, when forced by hunger, they should commit such an act, provided they came boldly forth and acknowledged it and offered remuneration.

A few miles further we came in sight of the Cheyenne village, located in a beautiful valley shaded by ancient cottonwoods. They seemed well provided with horses, which were scattered around quietly feeding. Most of the young men were absent, but an old chief came out to meet us. After a few questions regarding our route, we moved on in order to get out of their reach. Three miles' travel brought us to a fine locality for our camp, in a large grove of tall cottonwoods by the side of a natural meadow which afforded a sufficiency of good grass for our animals.

Saw today many birds such as are common in the east; several varieties of woodpeckers and the meadow lark were very abundant. We determined our position to be in latitude 37° 51′ 59″, longitude 103° 25′ 30″.

Monday, 18th.—We waited here the best part of the day for our beeves which we had left at

---

7. Garrard, in *Wah-To-Yah, and the Taos Trail* (1850), p. vi, says that in pronouncing the Indian name "the accent is on the second syllable." The Spanish Peaks were much remarked by early travelers on the Santa Fe Trail south of Bent's Fort.

Bent's Fort, for we feared lest they should return, knowing our route would thus a second time bring us so near. Some of our old Cheyenne friends came to our camp. At first they did not recognise us, and began a repetition of some of their dances, which they thought best adapted to awaken our benevolent feelings. Not succeeding, they begged and stole a few small things, and left us. My friend Shonka-mah-to was amongst them and seemed delighted to meet us again. He offered to present me his moccasins, which were very handsomely worked with beads. In this country they are obliged to sole them to protect the feet against the numerous cacti; these soles are of parflèche, the inside edge cut perfectly straight and the toe pointed.

In the afternoon our men arrived; and Hatcher, our hunter, also came with them, bringing a fine fat buck which he had killed on the way. A part of it was soon smoking on our rural-spread board beneath the cottonwoods; which despatched, we resumed our march. The approaching cliffs now narrowed the riverbed into what is termed, in the language of the country, a cañon, and precluded, for the present, further attempts to follow the river through the bottom. The high escarpments of rocks, rising on either side to the height of one or two hundred feet, form a sort of chasm through which the rapid current dashes over a succession of rocky ledges. These perpendicular walls are broken into numerous ravines impassable by wagons; and some of them, extending far into the plain, made it necessary for us to keep at a great distance from the river or to make continued detours to avoid them. We made 7 miles over this rough road and camped at the head of a dry fork where we found a small pool of water under a rock, but it was so highly impregnated with common salt and sulphate of soda as to be nauseous and bitter to the taste. Our cattle having had a long drive from Bent's, in addition to our march, rested quietly without any idea of making their escape.

Tuesday, August 19th.—Leaving the Purgatory some miles to our left, we stretched away nearly due west, following the valley of the dry fork in a direction nearly parallel with the Arkansas, whose heavily timbered margin lay on our right hand in clear view. At length we ascended a steppe, following a winding path through the rounded sand buttes which lie on its immediate flanks: though apparently perfectly level when viewed from below, we found, as we traversed it, that it was roughened by a succession of sandy rolls covered with artemisia [sagebrush], Yucca angustifolia [soap plant], and a species of cactus, Cactus peruvianus. The latter plant has a hard woody stem and numerous branches covered with long and sharp spines. As the plant rises to the height of 4 or 5 feet, the Mexican Spaniards frequently set them out in rows to form hedges for the protection of their fields. On our left the distant bluffs were capped with a species of cedar which by its deep green formed an agreeable contrast with the brown and barren soil on which it grew.

On the elevated plains we often met with extensive villages of the prairie dog, Arctomys ludoviciana. I was thrown from my horse in endeavouring to shoot one. Being determined to kill him, I laid the reins on my horse's neck that I might have both hands to steady my gun. As my horse had passed some distance beyond him, I was obliged to turn very much out of my seat; the report of the gun startled the horse; my spur, getting entangled between the saddle flaps and his side, rendered it impossible for me to quiet him; and, after a series of plunges, I was precipitated amongst the burrows of my intended victims. The prairie dog raises a hillock about 6 inches high by throwing out the dirt from the burrows, which are run very obliquely in order to prevent the rain from beating in. This animal is of a fawn color, and in form resembles a large squirrel, except the tail, which is about 3 inches long and destitute of long hair, curved slightly upwards. Their ears look as though they had been cut off close to the head. Like all gregarious animals, their social relations are very systematic and interesting. Some appear to possess great rank, whilst others act in the capacity of sentinels and always give notice of the approach of danger, for they have numerous enemies amongst the wolves as well as the human race. Rattlesnakes and burrowing owls—Strix cunicularia—live in the same burrows. These animals apparently dwell together in great harmony; but as we often found the snakes distended by the young dogs they had swallowed, we inferred that they at least frequented the dog towns from some other motive than that of disinterested friendship.

Hatcher tells me that they often disappoint the hunter when approaching the deer, for the moment the dog barks the deer bounds off. They are frequently shot by the men, who consider them a great delicacy. They have a very sprightly bark, which Dr. Harlan says may be imitated by pronouncing the syllable "cheh, cheh, cheh," in a sibilated manner, and in rapid succession, by propelling the breath between the tip of the tongue and the roof of the mouth.[8] Each sound they utter is accompanied by a flourish of the tail and jerk of the body. Like all of the marmot family, they are said to spend the cold season in a lethargic state. Cuvier says they protect themselves in winter by closing up the entrance of their burrows and make a nest of a globular form of dry grass,[9] having a small aperture at the top and so compact that they may be rolled about without receiving injury. When anyone approaches, they retreat into their burrows, keeping up an incessant barking. They live on the vegetation, and are extremely cleanly.

As we stopped for a few moments, a fine jet-black wild horse, or "mustang,"[10] came dashing up to camp, mistaking us probably for the herd to which he belonged. Throwing his head in the air, he gazed at us a few moments and, having discovered his mistake, turned from us and trotted off, leaving a column of dust as he disappeared to seek his companions in the valley below. We saw several fine antelope. In endeavoring to approach one I got my feet full of the spines of the prickly pear, for I happened to have moccasins which were not soled.

3. Timpa Valley · Santa Fe Trail · Raton Fork · Imposing Scenery

After 6 hours' travel we reached the banks of the Timpa, a creek of minor importance, which falls into the Arkansas 12 or 14 miles above Bent's Fort. It was nearly dry when we reached it, only a little water being discovered in pools which had been protected from the rays of the sun by the high banks. The Timpa flows through a beautiful valley, also one of erosion, varying in width from half a mile to a mile, but entirely destitute of timber. Through the valley passes a trail, but recently commenced, leading from Bent's Fort to Taos and Santa Fe. Striking this road we soon came to a pool of water, which began to be much needed by the animals. Standing by the side of the pool was an ox which had either strayed from, or had been left by, some party of traders. He joined himself to our little band of cattle, and we traveled along the trail 3 or 4 miles further, when we reached an old camping ground where we remained for the night, having then traveled 25 miles. As there was no timber, we were forced to use the artemisia as a substitute, which grew so luxuriantly as to be almost impenetrable. We found it answered very well, burning with a slight crackling and a clear flame. The water was again bitter, though more palatable than that of the previous evening.

Wednesday, August 20th.—We have now a fine road and progress rapidly along the side of the Timpa. The water is in pools, for the drought this year has been great. On the left side we have sand hills covered with cedars; the country generally much broken, except in the neighborhood of the road; at length the cliffs become quite precipitous. On the west side of the valley, and through the opening, we caught an occasional glimpse of the neighboring mountains.

Crossing a spur of the bluff which projects into the valley, we saw beyond a line of willows which marked the winding course of the main branch of the Timpa, and we argued from the widening of

---

8. *Fauna Americana* (1825), p. 162.

9. Cf. *Cuvier's Animal Kingdom* (London, 1840), p. 111.

10. There seems to have been in modern times no true wild horse except Prjévalski's species in central Asia. The mustang is wild in the sense that, being ownerless and unbroken, it runs wild and maintains itself in its environment. Its earliest American forebears were horses belonging to Spaniards, perhaps at or near Santa Fe (see Francis Haines, "Where Did the Plains Indians Get Their Horses?" *American Anthropologist*, n.s., Vol. 40 [1938], pp. 112–117); and its name is traced to the Spanish terms *mesteño* and *mostrenco*, which indicate its "lost, strayed, or stolen" condition. In the course of time, strayed horses of other than Spanish blood have variously mixed the stock.

the valley a continuation of fine traveling. On the western side the bluffs for a time seemed to disappear, and in their place we saw a fine plain covered with green grass extending for 8 or 10 miles towards the mountains. The bluffs on the left hand were deeply indented by numerous valleys and crowned with cedars. Here we found great abundance of the common [deer], Cervus virginianus, also black-tailed deer, Cervus macrotis. We succeeded in procuring a plentiful supply. The artemisia was literally alive with a large species of gray hare, Lepus americanus.

On reaching the bed of the stream we found it perfectly dry, and it was not until late in the day that we came to a place which showed signs that recently a party of traders in advance of us had camped there. At the foot of a ledge of rocks we found an abundance of water; but it was warm from exposure to the sun, and bitter, as heretofore.

The day had been exceedingly warm, but the moment the sun sunk below the horizon the temperature suddenly fell, so that before the morning we were suffering with cold. A hundred yards below our camp the stream passed through a cañon 75 feet deep. On examination we found the rock which had been cut through was brown sandstone, highly ferruginous, and the disintegration of the rocks had left thousands of small spherical and ellipsoidal nodules of iron. One of the wagon tires came off during the day, the dryness of the atmosphere having caused the wood to shrink. We bound it on with strips of rawhide and drove horseshoe nails in the felloes to prevent any lateral motion of the tire. Shortly after, finding the body of an old Spanish "carreta" by the roadside, it was burnt and the scraps of iron appropriated. We obtained from it suitable spike nails for the tire.

The cacti were very numerous; among which we saw the Cactus opuntia, a kind resembling a small cantelope half hidden in the ground, C. melocactus [Melocactus communis], and the C. peruvianus, before mentioned as used for forming hedges. The stems, when old, are extremely hard and resemble the woodwork carved by the South Sea Islanders. The foliage of the cedar trees around our camp presents the appearance of an oblate spheroidal mass, not otherwise differing from the common Juniperus virginianus. We saw the migratory robin, Turdus migratorius, flying about in search of the berries, which were sufficiently abundant to feed hosts of birds. A plant called "Adam's needle," Yucca angustifolia, was very abundant. The remarkable beauty of its conspicuous spike of campanulate flowers has procured it the name of the "prairie lighthouse"; the Spaniards call it the "palmilla." At noon we stopped a short time to water the animals without suffering them to be ungeared. We found it refreshed them very much and caused but little delay, which was well repaid by the renewed vigor of our march.

We are now in latitude 37° 38′ 25″, longitude 104° 35′ 22″.

Thursday, August 21st.—The nature of the country at first forced us into an order of travel which we now adopted from choice. It had been our practice to start at daylight, stopping a few hours during the heat of the day and continuing our journey in the cool of the evening. We now remained in camp until the mules had grazed for an hour or two; then starting, we completed our day's march before ungearing. It was afterwards acknowledged that this method of traveling enabled us to accomplish the same distance with much less fatigue to man and beast. On setting out from camp we found ourselves again pent up between two walls of rock. On the roadside we saw numerous specimens of the Mirabilis jalapa and collected some of the seed. Murray, the geographer, says that the true jalap is not obtained from this plant, but from the "purga de Xalapa," convolvulus which climbs to a considerable height and delights in cool, shady situations.[11]

11. Cf. *The Encyclopædia of Geography*, rev. ed. (Philadelphia, 1840), Vol. III, p. 314. The "true jalap" is the dried and powdered root of a plant (*Exogonium jalapa*) grown near Jalapa, Mexico. Spanish explorers learned from native Indians its cathartic powers and made it known in Europe, where in the era of "heroic medication" the drug was widely used for purging. It has also been used in the treatment of dropsy. The ninth edition of the *Encyclopædia Britannica* (1878) thought it worth noting that the average annual importation into Great Britain then amounted to 180,000 pounds. In more recent times its popularity has diminished. Today, mention of it is sooner found in old novels than in apothecaries' lists.

Seven miles from camp we came to what is called "Hole in the Rock," a place where water is to be found at all seasons. We stopped a few minutes to refresh our animals and had a pleasant rest under the cool shade of the densely foliaged cedar trees. On tasting the water [we] found it pure and sweet, being entirely free from the bitter taste which characterized the water of the stream lower down. This was the best water we had found in the valley of the Timpa. Three hours after leaving this place we reached the summit of the dividing ridge between the waters of the Arkansas and Purgatory. We now entered a beautiful level plain, and again gazed with admiration on the grand peaks of the Wah-To-Yah, which seemed quite near; whilst beyond, in the gray distance, lay a long line of rugged peaks still marked near their summits with white lines of snow, which also filled the ravines that descended their sides. We soon received other proofs of our vicinity to the mountains. A severe hailstorm, with thunder and rain, burst upon us. We had some terrific claps and several sharp flashes of lightning, and the air soon became so chilled as to make our limbs quiver with the cold. The storm soon, however, passed off, and the sun again breaking forth, our clothes quickly dried. Such storms are of frequent occurrence in the region of the mountains, where the clouds are constantly forming by the warm currents of the plains' meeting with the cool moisture-condensing atmosphere which hangs around the summits of these snow-capped mountains.

After a march of 24 miles, the last of which lay in the extended plain, we encamped at a place called "Hole in the Prairie," a low marshy spot, from which several little creeks seem to derive their existence. There was no wood except a few willows, and the tall coarse grass afforded but little nourishment to our hungry animals.

August 22nd.—After the first mile the road began to descend into the valley of the Purgatory. We soon reached a sand plain of 3 or 4 miles in width which we had to pass before crossing the stream. We forded the river with some difficulty (for the banks were quite steep) and then proceeded along the road, which led over a rough and broken country. On the right bank we encamped just at the point where the stream issues from the mountains, at which point its valley is palisaded by rocks 1500 feet high whose tops form a vast plain and whose strata are so similar that one cannot for a moment doubt that this elevated plateau once extended unbroken over the present wide valley of the stream. The river continues well timbered, the cottonwood still being the characteristic sylva, amongst which we also found the black walnut. The shrubbery consists chiefly of the plum, cherry, and currant.

Lieut. Peck had quite an adventurous chase after his mule, which made his escape while he was engaged in getting plums which hung in tempting clusters near the river. I cannot do better than give the adventure in his own words. He says: "Invited by a bush loaded with fine plums, I alighted for a moment to gather some, leaving my mule attached to the bush; on [my] turning to remount, he became frightened and started at full speed towards our last night's camp. I followed as fast as a pedestrian can make his way over the cactus-strewed plain, but the animal was gaining so fast that I soon gave up the hope of overtaking him. Hatcher, who, like myself, was in advance of the party, discovering my plight, plied whip and spur to cut off his retreat, but his dull mule was soon left behind. Passing the main body of the caravan, three or four of the best horsemen joined in the chase, now becoming more and more exciting. As our sketchbook containing notes of the route to this point was attached to the saddle, I felt some anxiety for its safety and, mounting the first mule at hand, followed in the wake of the pursuers. After 6 miles the hand of a skilful 'laryetto' noosed the recreant beast, and we all returned to camp well pleased with our Gilpin-like mule chase, and with the book safe."

Hatcher killed four black-tailed deer, Cervus macrotis. They bear a great resemblance to the common deer, the chief distinctive mark being a black tip at the end of the tail. At the crossing, one of the men shot a large red-tailed hawk, Falco borealis. The river is here 15 yards wide, about

To wck lii...

Shon-ka-nah-to

1 foot in depth, and with a current of 5 or 6 miles per hour. As we passed along the bluffs, in many places overhanging the bottoms, we saw them covered with the yellow flowers of the helianthi [sunflowers], amongst whose brilliant clusters the frightened deer, ever and anon, sprang from his lair. The wild turkey, Meleager gallopavo, too would frequently enliven our route, dashing rapidly across our path to take shelter in the neighboring thicket. Although very abundant, yet they formed no object of pursuit, being at this season very lean.

The bottom in which we camped was filled with black locust. We were struck with the quantity of dead timber on the riverside. Its situation led us to conclude that it might have been destroyed by some great rise of the waters. The hop vine, Humulus lupulus, is found here in great abundance. The sides of the valleys as far as the eye can reach are bounded by high precipitous cliffs, many of which are entirely shrouded with the sombre foliage of the cedar.

Robins and flickers, Picus auratus, flitting gaily around, give life and animation to the scene. The last-named bird is remarkable on account of the singular disposition of the roots of its tongue, which, passing along on either side of the neck towards the back of the skull, join on the top of the head and are continued as far as the root of the upper mandible. Wilson remarks that in one species of the Picus it is wound round the orbital bone of the right eye, which projects considerably more than the left, for its accommodation.[12] There was also a jay whose plumage partook of the colour of the darkest blue of a clear sky, but in manner, size, and disposition, bears a striking resemblance to our common blue jay, and like the latter it is fond of imitating and ridiculing other birds. I sometimes amused myself by repeating some of their notes, whereupon they would dart off in great rage, appearing to be most furiously incensed, manifesting the same feelings as a human being who possesses the same propensity of ridiculing others. We also found here the magpie, Corvus pica, in great abundance, and they were daily seen as long as we continued in this beautiful valley, but as soon as we left it we lost sight of them.

The night was very clear and we obtained some fine observations, which placed us in latitude 37° 11′ 02″, longitude 104° 35′ 22″.

August 23rd.—We continued to follow the valley for two or three miles further, when the approaching rocks forced the trail into a defile formed by an affluent of the Purgatory. As we entered this dell we could trace the Purgatory valley for several miles by the light silvery green of the cottonwood foliage, until at last further view was intercepted by an intervening mountain.

Our road now became exceedingly rough, leading along a tortuous valley, sometimes passing on one side of the Raton Fork, sometimes on the other, whilst occasionally the narrowness of the banks forced us to seek a passage in the rocky bed of the creek itself. Traveling in the deep ravine of a mountain stream, our horses' feet splashed in its cool waters, so tempting that the ferns bent forward to lave their dark fronds in the limpid stream. Luxuriant vines, and trees of healthiest green, formed arbours for our heads. It appeared like passing through tunnels formed by the goddess Flora, and we looked around as if expecting to see the Naiads of the Purgatory spring from some nook in the moss-covered banks. We were almost wild with excitement. Having suffered so much from drinking the nauseous salt water of the plains, we could have wished for the days of the Metamorphosis and prayed to be changed into one of these cool mountain streams. Although sheltered from the sun, when we gazed upward we beheld the flicker with golden wings gliding above and glistening in his brilliant rays. And sometimes as we crossed a high dividing ridge we caught sight of the towering summits of the Wah-To-Yah. As we proceeded, we noticed on either side groves of pine and cedar; willows and aspens lined the creek, and in one place we found a scattering grove of oaks.

Although the scenery charmed us, the roughness of the road had quite a different effect on our

12. *Wilson's American Ornithology* (Boston, 1840), p. 103.

jaded mules, and after a toilsome ascending march of 7 miles we were glad to reach a wide valley which afforded an inviting location for our camp. The open space was covered with high grass, and we all drank immense draughts of the cool crystal water of the mountain stream, rendered peculiarly grateful when contrasted with the fluid with which we had been obliged to assuage our thirst for the last 5 or 6 days.

Hatcher shot me one of those beautiful jays which I first saw yesterday; since, I have found it described by Audubon as the Corvus ultramarinus. We also saw the species of pine, Pinus monophylla, which contains in its cone a number of eatable nuts nearly as large as the kernels of the groundnut. I brought in some of the cones, which are remarkably resinous. In the appendix to Capt. Frémont's report of 1843 and 1844 there is a botanical description of this tree. We found them generally from 30 to 40 feet in height and bearing such a resemblance to the common pine that one might easily pass them without noticing any difference. We collected and ate many of the nuts and found them exceedingly pleasant to the taste. Gregg says that considerable quantities are exported annually to the southern cities and that they are sometimes used for the manufacture of oil which may be used as a substitute for lamp oil.[13] They form the chief article of food of the Pueblos and New Mexicans.

Among the plants we noticed the blue larkspur, Delphinium, which resembles the cultivated kind except the interior of the corolla, which presents a pubescent appearance; the wild geranium, Geranium maculatum; the beautiful flowering flax, Linum perenne; also a delicate harebell, Campanula linifolia, which I have found as far north as the Manitou Islands of Lake Michigan; also a beautiful scarlet flower (Convolvulaceæ).

Shortly after forming our camp, whilst I was sitting on the ground completing a sketch, a large bull snake at least 5 feet in length crawled from beneath me. Yount and Patrick [Bradley] started in pursuit of the "monstrum horrendum," but the snake managed to escape unscathed. During the afternoon some of our people made an excursion to a peak which, owing to the peculiar clearness of the atmosphere of the country, appeared very near, but the excursion proved much longer and more toilsome than they had anticipated. They described the surface of the country which met their view as perfectly flat, here and there varied by beautiful lakes. The night being clear, we observed, and found our latitude 37° 1′ 33″, longitude 104° 37′ 32″.

I cannot conclude the day without again alluding to the scenery. Every moment, our eyes were arrested by the imposing grandeur of the precipitous cliffs which walled us in on either side, and the beautiful stream which danced along from rock to rock, whilst continually several small rivulets, borne from the cool springs of the mountainside, burst from the dark dells where they seemed to lurk and joined in the merry dance of the crystal waters. There was not one in our party who did not feel well repaid for the trying hardships he had endured on the sandy wastes of the prairie. I thought that the pleasure afforded us, as with delighted eye we gazed around, seemed not inferior to that experienced whilst looking on the falling waters of Niagara.

We took numerous sketches, upon which the magnetic bearing and the hours of the day are noted; they will therefore present more exact scenographical ideas than any description could possibly convey and will assist in defining the rapid outlines we made of the geological features of this country. Many prominences of great magnitude that day after day imposed their grandeur upon us were frequently delineated, but we have thought it best to suppress all but one of each different scene. Some of them will possess a peculiar interest in a country destitute of landmarks, where every irregularity acquires in consequence a great value.

---

13. Gregg, *Commerce of the Prairies* (1844), Vol. I, chap. vii.

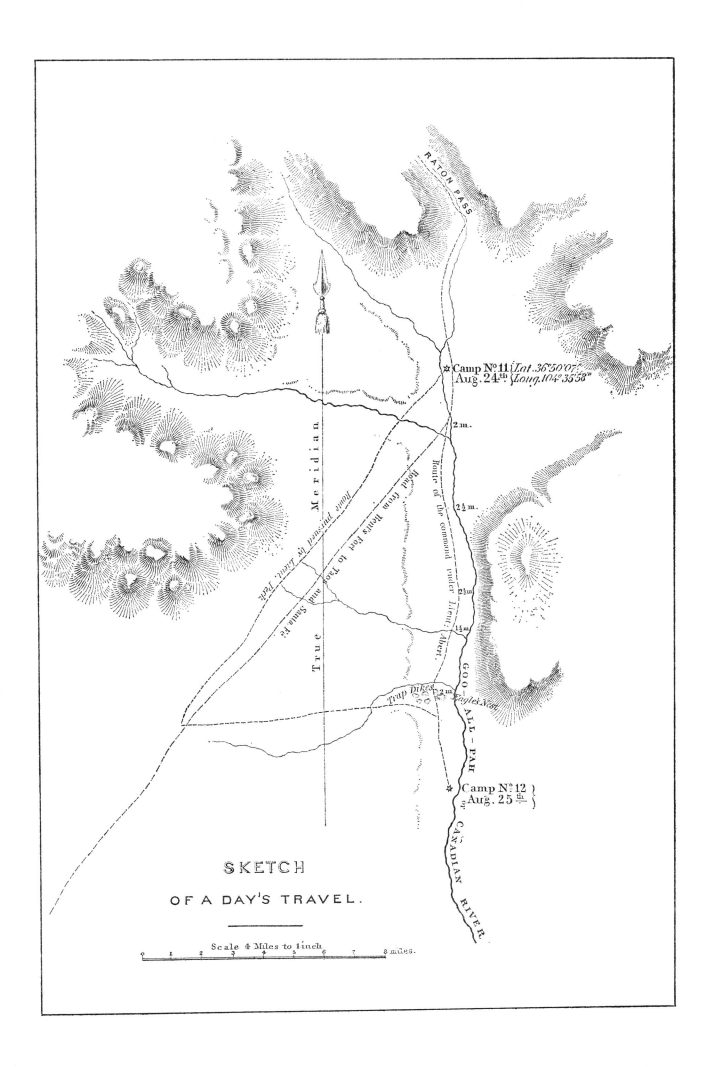

RATON PASS

☆ Camp Nº 11 {Lat. 36°50'07"
Aug. 24ᵗʰ {Long. 104°35'58"

2 m.

Meridian

2½ m.

Route pursued by Lieut. Peck

Road from Bents Fort to Taos and Santa Fe

Route of the command under Lieut. Abert

2½ m.

True

1½ m.

Trap Dikes

2 m.

Eagles Nest

GOO - ALL - PAH

☆ Camp Nº 12 }
Aug. 25ᵗʰ }

CAÑADIAN RIVER

SKETCH

OF A DAY'S TRAVEL.

Scale 4 Miles to 1 inch

0 1 2 3 4 5 6 7 8 miles.

"O-cum-who-wust"

Chief of the Cheyennes. aug 45

4. Through the Raton Pass · Beginnings of the Canadian · Bears

Sunday, August 24th.—On leaving our last night's camp we ascended a hill 3 miles, to the summit of the mountain spur known by the name of the "Raton." A splendid view suddenly burst upon us as we reached the point most elevated in the whole route. We had expected to see the valley of the Canadian, but, looking to the south, could discern nothing but a confused mass of rock, whilst on our right the Spanish Peaks again welcomed us, asserting their supremacy above the long, many-headed range of the Sierra Blanca, which, gradually dwindling, stretched off to the south as far as the eye could reach.

Turning into the valley which led down the mountain, we found it at first more open than the one we had ascended the day previous; but it soon became narrower and steeper, so that we had considerable difficulty in getting our wagons over the rough and rock-strewed road. The many fragments of wagons, such as hounds and axletrees, proved that those who had preceded us found it no less difficult. Where the ravine widened we found quantities of cherries, Cerasus virginianus, but the bushes dwarfed by the rocky soil.

At 11 o'clock we emerged from the gorge and entered a small prairie or park engirdled by mountains. When we first caught sight of this green valley, its fresh appearance led us to expect a fine camping ground, but on passing over the sandy plains we found the grass coarse and thinly scattered over the surface. We pitched our tents in a bend of the stream which forms the principal source of the Canadian, or "Goo-al-pah,"[14] as it is called by the Kioways and Comanches. The soil of the valley is not very good, appearing sandy and barren, except on the banks of the stream, where the luxuriant herbage indicates more depth and fertility. The cacti again appeared, and the bottom was filled with the tall sunflower (Heliantheæ), where the deer and the turkey found shelter from the warm rays of the sun.

We have now finally crossed the Reton ("Retoño" of the Spaniards),[15] which is the only difficult part of the regular route to Santa Fe by the way of Bent's Fort, which we concluded to be the preferable road at all times, in which opinion we are confirmed by finding it the route most traveled this year. It is, however, 60 miles further; but the beauty of the scenery, the delightful freshness of the snow-cooled water of the mountains, with good grass and timber in abundance, give it greatly the superiority; whilst, by the lower route, yon travel, according to the information of Mr. J. N. Simpson, 50 miles to Sand Creek, which is generally dry, then 118 miles to McNees's Creek; although water can generally be procured in the Cimarron, 70 miles from Sand Creek, by digging in the bed of the river, which is extremely inconvenient for watering the animals.

Whilst we were quietly eating our dinner, the guard discovered a large black bear, Ursus americanus, quite close to our camp. The alarm being given, many clutched their guns and started off in pursuit, but [they] soon returned unsuccessful. I heard here a singular story in reference to the bear, which story was corroborated by many of the old voyageurs in my party, who say that the female is never killed with young. As the anatomical structure of this animal is so similar to other mammiferous animals as to preclude the possibility of a dissimilar parturition, I at first gave but little credit to the story; but, having since found the same thing mentioned by Pennant,[16] have thought it worthy of notice. He accounts for the fact by supposing that the female bear remains concealed during the whole period of gestation and does not leave her retreat until the cubs are quite large, fearing that the males should devour them.

---

14. So spelled also on Abert's map, but further on in the journal it appears without the terminal "h."

15. In the journal entry for August 23, and on his map, Abert uses the customary spelling "Raton." His "Reton" and "Retoño" seem off the mark.

16 Cf. Thomas Pennant, *History of Quadrupeds*, 3rd ed. (London, 1793), Vol. II, pp. 2–3.

Our camp was in latitude 36° 50′ 07″, longitude 104° 35′ 58″, and about 4 miles from the point at which the stream issues from the mountains. At this place the bed of the stream is a few feet in width; our hunter said that two miles above it was entirely dry. Its water was exceedingly cold and clear.

5. Gold Country · Rattlesnakes · Grand Canyon of the Canadian

We have now reached a great mineral country; but, as no specimens fell immediately within our reach, we thought it unadvisable to venture into the mountain in a search which might prove unsuccessful and require our party to be delayed in a country where we were likely to be arrested by the government and deprived of all our notes and papers. Our people, however, often indulged in golden dreams, excited not a little by Hatcher's account of having procured a quantity of gold dust from a Pueblo Indian for a few charges of ammunition; and, as they listened eagerly, they looked as if they harbored serious intentions of returning to this Eldorado of the west.

Gold is found in almost every portion of New Mexico, and in some places silver, copper, lead, and zinc. Iron must be abundant, as all the rocks around present a highly ferruginous appearance, and we once observed, as has been previously stated, distinct seams of this metal traversing the sandstone in such a manner as to present the appearance of a mosaic pavement. The principal gold mines are in the vicinity of Santa Fe and Taos; but the method of working them pursued by the Spaniards and Pueblo Indians is so rude that we cannot form a fair estimate of their value. The opposition which [the Mexican] government offers to more skilful foreigners, for fear lest anyone else should share the wealth which the rapacious rulers wish to monopolize, prevents their being fairly tested. Although sometimes the power may be placed in the hands of liberal men, yet so unstable is the government, so uncertain the laws, that no one will venture capital under their protection. If, however, the United States succeed in inducing Mexico to admit the boundary of Texas as claimed, to the Río del Norte,[17] the enterprising people of our country, protected by our laws, will gladly invest their energy and capital in this business, and, with advantage of machinery such as has been used in our southern States, will no doubt reap rich rewards from a region celebrated, from the days of Montezuma, as a country of gold and silver.

Since leaving this country we have heard that the miners have been very successful and from 40 to 60 men were daily coming into Santa Fe. At Tuerto, Mr. Campbell, an American, has been engaged in working a "plassara" [placer] in which he found a piece of gold weighing 50 ounces. It is worth $19 per ounce, whilst that from the old plassara is $19.25 per oz. The dust is much sought after by the traders, as specie is liable to an export duty of 6 per cent.

August 25th.—Whilst preparing to continue our journey we were agreeably surprised at seeing a single horseman ride into our camp. He proved to be an American trader named Fisher and was on his way to Bent's Fort from Taos, with no other companion than his rifle. We were glad to see him, and he gave us useful information of the country through which we were to pass. His long residence in the Indian country made him about as familiar with the roads and passes as the Indians themselves. He told us to keep the left bank, as we should find the other impassable for our wagons, and we should probably suffer for water in passing the Grand Cañon [of the Canadian]. Whilst partaking of a prairie breakfast with us, he inquired the news from the United States, and in return gave such as he possessed. As he departed to prosecute his lonely journey we could but admire the boldness of character acquired by long exposure to danger and privation.

Whilst Mr. Fitzpatrick conducted the wagons and main party down the river, Lieut. Peck was directed to proceed with Mr. Hatcher along the base of the mountains, in order to make a more

---

17. The Rio Grande, now the principal boundary line between the United States and Mexico.

detailed examination of the valley; [and] to examine the Vermejo, which unites with the Canadian 20 miles from its issue out of the mountains.

The valley here is 25 miles in width, and, though not so fertile as some of the lands in the Mississippi Valley, might by proper cultivation support a numerous population. It is well watered, and flanked on three sides by rocky barriers: on the north by the Raton spur of the Rocky Mountains, which we had just crossed; to the west are the high mountains of the Sierra Blanca, separating it from the valley of the Río del Norte; while the rugged cliffs or brows of the tableland limit it on the east.

Should our government succeed in extending its territory to the Río del Norte, this valley or park would form the most eligible site for a military post. By a small expenditure the pass through the mountains might be made into a good road and would then be traveled altogether and in preference to the lower route. This position is the more desirable as it is situated upon the trail of the Utah and other mountain Indians, who make continual incursions and attacks upon the "ranchos" of New Mexico. It would be about equidistant between Bent's Fort and Taos, and, with the contemplated posts along the Arkansas, would form a valuable strategic line controlling the whole country, particularly our possessions in Texas, whose northern frontier is much exposed to the depredations of the Kioways, Witchetahs, and Comanches.

Among the plants entitled to particular notice was Yucca angustifolia, "palmilla," or soap plant, which is seen in great abundance, not only in the valley, but along the high bluffs which form the grand cañon. Hatcher informed us that the root of this plant, when bruised and prepared, formed a substitute for soap and is used by the Pueblos and Spaniards, who prefer it for many purposes to soap itself.

Lieut. Peck and Hatcher joined us near some singular trap dikes, the highest of which is known by the name of Eagle's Nest, rising from 80 to 100 feet above the plain. We examined them particularly, and found them to consist of a series arranged in four perfectly parallel lines extending across the valley in a direction nearly at right angles with the course of the river, having a magnetic bearing of 10° south of west. The first and most northern tier were contained in a belt 200 yards in width and extended from the bluff quite to the river, whilst the fourth was scarcely distinguishable and a quarter of a mile further down the valley. The crumbling detritus from the decay of the upper portions had formed on either side the vertical wall a regular talus; and as we viewed them from the bluff they bore a strong resemblance to an embanked road which extended before us perfectly straight.

The manner of this formation seems plainly demonstrable. The matter of which the dike is composed, whilst in a molten state, has been thrown into those parallel fissures which are produced by violent subterraneous disturbances. As the descending water swept away the valley, the harder trap yielded not so readily, but must have presented the appearance of four parallel walls of uniform thickness extending across the valley, as the irresistible waters forced their way through, and continued action leveled the breaches with the present plain, leaving these fragments a monument of its mighty deeds.

The detritus has given to two of the lower ones in the northern series the appearance of rounded buttes, until viewed from above, when you see the singularly parallel lines before mentioned, plainly showing the original thickness of the dike. We ascended one of the highest, which presented to the north a vertical surface of a dark brown color. Upon examination we found it to be a pretty hard and compact green stone, crystallized in somewhat regular hexagonal prisms with their axes horizontal and perpendicular to the cooling surface. The absence of volcanic mounds and craters favours the supposition of a subterraneous injection of the fluid mass. From the top we had a fine view of the surrounding country, and Greenwood pointed out the most remarkable feature in the landscape, of which we obtained the magnetic bearings. Among the principal was Taos Mountain, which lay in a direction SW.

We were now approaching the junction of the Canadian and Vermejo and began to look for a crossing place, as we had been informed that the Vermejo was impassable by wagons on account of its high banks and soft bottom. We were unsuccessful in our search, therefore pitched our tents a few miles above the fork with the intention of cutting a path which would enable us to cross.

One of our mules was severely bitten by a rattlesnake, Crotalus horridus, and the leg became much swollen. We had him tied, thrown, and the wounded part scarified. In a few days he recovered, which is rather a proof that the means used alone saved the animal. Dr. Harlan, however, states that "perhaps not more than one case out of ten would prove mortal if left to nature."[18] Common hartshorn, or volatile alkali, has been regarded as an excellent remedy. The poor robin's plantain, Hieracium venosum, rattlesnake weed, a plant growing in dry woodlands, easily recognised by the colored veins of the leaf, has been used by persons exhibiting rattlesnakes, who freely suffer themselves to be bitten. The State of South Carolina some years ago purchased a secret antidote from a negro who in a nude state jumped into a tub filled with these snakes, in the presence of a number of persons, and, after being frequently bitten, entirely counteracted the effects of the poison by swallowing the expressed juice of a plant which proved to be water plantain, Alisma plantago, which can be easily recognised by its ovate acute leaf.[19]

It is said that its [the rattlesnake's] bite will poison its own body; and people who, when pressed with hunger, are often forced to eat these reptiles, are careful not to let them injure themselves with their teeth, but quickly separate the head from the body and thus get rid of all its poisonous effects. This precaution is probably unnecessary, as it has been stated that this poison is harmless when taken into the stomach.

August 26th.—Half an hour's search discovered a place where the river runs over a rocky bottom with alluvial banks 8 or 10 feet high. There was a little narrow path marked on both banks, showing it was the crossing place of the deer and other animals, whose sagacity always leads them to select the most advantageous crossing. All hands set to work with pick and spade, and in a few hours we enjoyed the satisfaction of seeing all our wagons safely over on the left bank of the Canadian. We now stretched away in a direction bearing a little west of south, passing over a sandy plain heated to a high temperature by the intense rays of the sun. We passed some "buttes," from the top of which we had a fine view of the winding course of the river as well as of the adjacent mountains.

We saw numbers of prairie dogs and rattlesnakes. The latter are said to be blind in the month of August. Being dangerous animals, we did not attempt to ascertain whether this is the case. They, however, never venture far from their holes, and commence rattling on hearing a footstep, without any apparent indication of knowledge as regards the direction of approach.

Shortly after passing the mouth of the Vermejo we saw slate bluffs of a fine quality, an indubitable proof of the existence of coal. Hatcher shot a fawn in sight of the party. We watched him, half screened in the tall reeds, as he again reloaded, for the doe was so attached to her fawn that she seemed quite reluctant to leave, but was gazing bewildered around; when again the rifle rings, and she too lay quivering in the agonies of death.

August 27th.—Today we made a march of 20 miles, again passing bluffs of shale similar to the slate we noticed the day previous. They are to be met with just before reaching the lower Santa Fe route, which we crossed about 10 o'clock. The point where it crosses the Canadian is called "El

---

18. Richard Harlan, M.D., *Medical and Physical Researches* (Philadelphia, 1835), p. 585.

19. *Ibid.*, pp. 491–492. Harlan tells the story, but guards himself by remarking that the persons present are "said to have" witnessed the efficacy of the remedy.

Vado de Piedras" [Rocky Ford] and is about 46 miles from the upper ford; quite near was the termination of a little ridge known as "Point of Rocks." The river, though increased by numerous affluents, is still but a few yards in width, with very little water.

At noon we reach the grand cañon, which is referred to by Gregg in his "Commerce of the Prairies" as a source of great annoyance to early travelers. He says: "In 1825, a caravan with a number of wagons reached it [about] 5 miles below the present ford. The party was carefully moving along without suspecting [even] a ravine at hand, as the bordering plains were exceedingly level, and the opposite margins of equal height, when suddenly they found themselves upon the [very] brink of an immense precipice, several hundred feet [yards] deep, and almost perpendicular on both sides of the river." He continues, in the words of Mr. Stanley: "We travelled fifty miles, the whole of which distance [the river] is bound in by cliffs several hundred feet high, in many places [nearly] perpendicular. We at length came to the termination of the tableland; but what a scene presented itself! The valley below could only be reached by descending a frightful cliff of from 1200 to 1500 feet, and more or less precipitous."[20] The exaggerated accounts of travelers, with numerous tales of suffering for want of water, made us somewhat cautious in proceeding; but, as we advanced, we became convinced that it was to be the most interesting part of our journey.

As we ascended the high ground we descried a train of Santa Fe wagons which had stopped to noon on a small creek four or five miles to the eastward of us. Anxious to hear from the United States, we despatched a messenger to them. On his return he reported the proprietors of the train to be Dr. Conelly [Connelley], Dr. East, Mr. McGuffin [Magoffin], and an English gentleman whose name he did not ascertain. They had left the States but a few days after our departure and had neither papers nor intelligence. They had forty-two wagons, most of them capable of carrying 5000 lbs. The wagons are made large on account of the duty being charged per wagon. Having followed the regular trail of the Cimarron, they had experienced great difficulty in procuring water, often having been obliged to dig for it in the sandy beds of the rivers; nor did their difficulties end here, for information has since reached us that the duties had been raised to 750 dollars per wagon, and 150 for translating the "manifesto" [into Spanish] and that the regulation confiscating cotton goods as contraband had been rigidly enforced.

We camped at the head of a ravine about 4 miles from the river and about the same distance from the Santa Fe road. Our astronomical observations placed us in latitude 36° 12' 35.8", longitude 104° 26' 52".

We saw great numbers of the [pronghorn] antelope, Dicranocerus furcifer, one band containing nearly fifty. It has sometimes been called "antilocapra," but to this Cuvier[21] offers an objection, for which he quotes the authority of Fabricius, "Nomina hybrida nullo modo toleranda." He says the female has horns. As we had not seen them with horns, Mr. Fitzpatrick was applied to for information. He says "they have horns, but it is not a general thing, as by far the greater number have none." They are very graceful and wonderfully fleet, not bounding high like the deer, but running close to the ground, "ventre à terre"; neither do they raise the tail, but spread it in fan form. They do not turn the head in running, but, the body keeping the same level, they seem to glide away like spirits, so quickly do they disappear. Their hair is short and stiff, of a fawn color, except on the buttocks, belly, and tail, which are white; horns black, and remarkable for their base

---

20. Quoted from Gregg's *Commerce of the Prairies* (1844), Vol. II, chap. x. In the same volume, chap. iii, Gregg called the valley of the Canadian "one of the most magnificent sights I ever beheld," and continued with a description of it in the same vein.

21. *The Animal Kingdom* (London, 1827–1835), Vol. IV, pp. 167–168, 170–172. Joh. Chr. Fabricius, the Danish taxonomist, was against mixing Greek and Latin in scientific names; see, e.g., his *Philosophia entomologica* (1778), p. 107, "Nomina," sec. 18.

taking its origin directly over the eye, which is large, round, and projecting. Although excessively shy, they become so bewildered by fear, or at times so excited by curiosity, as to rush boldly within reach of the rifle. They are often enticed within shooting distance by displaying a handkerchief on the end of a wiping stick. When in the neighborhood of the buffalo one can without difficulty approach quite near: then, however, no one wishes to destroy them, for the former afford meat of finer flavor and in much greater quantity.

Deer are numerous in the bottom, often spring up quite close, and, raising their snowy tails, turn their heads round to gaze on us, giving them a gentle motion like the vibration of a pendulum, as if to rail at us, then bound away. The Indians raise the forefinger and imitate the motion of the tail when they wish to designate the deer. We are now nightly surrounded by a species of the wolf known as the prairie wolf [coyote], Canis latrans. The old voyageurs manifest great reluctance to injure the "medicine wolf," as they call them, on account of some superstitious notions which they have imbibed from continued association with the Indians.

August 28th.—We started this morning with the intention of making a short march in order to give the animals a good rest, for they appear much jaded. Lieut. Peck made an excursion to the river and great cañon through which it flows, and from which is derived the name Canada, or Canadian River.[22] As we were separated for the greater part of the day, I think it best for each to state what he saw in his own words. Lieut. Peck proceeds as follows:

"In approaching, we kept between two deep and impassable ravines, following the elevated tongue of land. Within half a mile of the brink the ground became so broken that we were obliged to dismount and scramble over the rocks on foot; at last we arrived at a point of a brow of the precipice which commanded a view of the deep chasm below us. From the exaggerated accounts, we had been prepared to see a channel of 1500 feet deep, and were somewhat disappointed in finding it little more than a sixth part of that depth. It was, however, sufficiently deep to excite our admiration and impress us with an idea of the wonderful effect of running water. The rock had been furrowed to the depth of 250 feet, nearly perpendicular, and the craggy sides were everywhere covered with cedars and pines that had caught root in the crevices. At the foot and between the two precipices lay a smiling valley, covered with a luxuriant growth of fresh grass through which in silent beauty the stream wound its way from bluff to bluff. A detached rock started a deer, and, as he bounded from his covert, broke in upon the dream in which I was indulging on the unbroken solitude of the scene before me. Just in front of where I was standing, a bend of the river had formed a magnificent cylindrical wall 200 feet in perpendicular height and as perfect as though the work of art. The rock is the same as above, viz. brown sandstone, and so soft as to yield easily to the effects of water."

Our caravan wended its way slowly along, being obliged to keep some distance from the river in order to avoid the little tributary cañons which would otherwise have proved continually barriers to our progress; and the detour we should have been obliged to make in order to head them would have caused great disparity between the distance traveled over and our actual progression. The road, too, was rendered extremely rough by a species of dry grass which grew in tussocks so hard that it was like traveling over a road strewed with brickbats. The country was growing dry and sterile. We, however, found a few large shallow pools covered with flocks of ducks, among

22. Abert's report printed as a Congressional Document reads thus. The Archives manuscript reads "Cañada, or Cañadian," with the tilde, which apparently was Abert's preference. The origin of the river's name is in dispute; some derive it from *canadien* because French Canadians were early in that region, for example the Mallet brothers and their companions, who traveled overland from above the Platte River to Santa Fe in 1739 and were on the Canadian River in canoes in 1740: see Margry's *Découvertes*, Vol. VI, chap. xii, and Henry Folmer, "The Mallet Expedition," *Colorado Magazine*, Vol. XVI (1939), pp. 161–173. Others trace the name to *cañada* because the river has a noteworthy valley: see Coues's 1895 edition of Pike's *Explorations*, Vol. II, p. 558 n.

which were the green-winged teal, Anas crecca. We also saw the killdeer plover, Charadrius vociferus, the [long-billed] curlew, Numenius longirostris, and a specimen of the American avoset,
Recurvirostra americana, the only one of the kind observed on our route. It appeared perfectly un-
acquainted with the destructive propensities of man; stood quietly, with its long legs half immersed
in the water, regardless of the approach of our people, who were on all sides of the pond, endeavouring to kill some of the ducks which were quietly gliding on its surface. We afterwards passed several
of these ponds in the open prairie; there have evidently been heavy rains here lately.

6. Open Prairie · Hailstorm · Antelope · Mustangs · Autumnal Flowers

Although we had endeavoured to keep well out from the river, we suddenly came upon a cañon
which extended some distance into the prairie. While the caravan followed it up in order to head it,
I went across, the better to keep our bearings, and was sitting under some cedar trees filling up the
sketch of the route when I heard the sharp ring of the rifle and, shortly after, the clattering of hoofs
on the hard rocks. 'Twas but a moment, when a large doe came bounding by. I gave her a passing
shot, but without effect, then mounted my mule and struck towards our trail. I found that Hatcher
had just killed an otter, Lutra canadensis. He had seen several in the pools which lay in the bottom
of the cañon, but only succeeded in getting this one.

Not long after, [we] having joined the camp, and whilst [we were] crossing a sandy reach, a small
black cloud which had been lowering in the east suddenly enlarged and burst upon us with all the
fury of a hungry tiger. The storm was terrific. The thunder crashed as if new cañons had been
riven. Hailstones as large as musket balls came in profusion, pouring down obliquely and driven by
the force of a strong wind. Many endeavoured to shelter themselves from the pitiless pelting by
taking refuge under the lee of the wagons, which were scattered about in all directions, for the
mules became ungovernable; but, finding an attempt to escape from the storm useless, the leaders
turned completely round in order to be sheltered by those behind. My mule was one of the most
whimsical in the band and commenced moving about as if she thought *I* was pelting her with the
hailstones. Ever and anon she would wince as one struck her in some very sensitive part of the
body; when at length, taxed beyond endurance, she humped her back like an angry cat. Knowing
what would follow such a demonstration, I quickly dismounted and took shelter under her lee.
What a situation!

The hailstones had piled up so as to form dams between the tussocks of reed grass, and the rain
which accompanied them caused the hard ground to be covered ankle-deep in water, while the hail
which whitened the prairie was one and a half inches deep. Many of the hailstones did not melt
until next morning. It would have been a laughable scene to a disinterested looker-on, if I may
judge from the effect a rude sketch produced on an untutored Indian. But *we* could not enjoy it.
We had been drenched to the skin, and the reduction of temperature which suddenly followed was
so great that we were nearly frozen.

The storm was over in less than an hour. We had been looking for water, that we might encamp.
Instead of dry ravines, we now found impassable torrents, and as they bore along in their rapid
currents huge fragments of fallen rock we readily conceived the manner in which the deep channels
had been excavated. With some difficulty we succeeded in passing one of the shallow streams and
formed our camp on a rock above. As there was a little dry grass in a neighboring valley, we concluded to remain; and by the means of a few moist rags which we sprinkled with powder, and a part
of the inside of an old log which had not been wet by the rain, we were soon enabled to light our
campfire, when the huge piles of dead cedar which we had heaped upon it sent forth a genial heat.
We again began to recover our spirits; and as we sat by our fires contemplating the well-loaded
roasting sticks (from an ox which had been killed upon the occasion) unusual cheerfulness pervaded

the assembly, and the glad song which arose that evening banished all remembrance of the afternoon's mishap.

Although we had purposed making a short march, we traveled 25 miles, and were now a short distance below the junction of the Canadian and the Moro [Mora]. The bluffs on the margin of the Canadian are covered with the pine and cedar.

August 29th.—Made a short march of 10 miles in order to give our animals time to recruit after the severe journey of yesterday, having passed over a distance of 25 miles. In a hard, flat depression of the prairie which looked as if it was sometimes covered with water we saw great numbers of antelope. Hatcher, who was some distance in advance of the main body, had dismounted and crept cautiously toward them; soon a little cloud of smoke was seen, which enlarged with the quickness of thought; at the same instant the antelope dashed off in all directions, leaving one weltering in his gore, and the report of the rifle faintly reached our ears. We soon arrived at the scene of slaughter; one of the wagons stopped, and the antelope was thrown in. Not long after, we saw a band of seven wild horses, or mustangs, whose appearance we had expected, having seen large heaps of their manure; they stood in a close group and for a long time intently watched our approach; at length, when [we were] quite near, they raised their long tails, shook their flowing manes, and dashed gracefully off. Our jaded mules looked anxiously after them, and doubtless envied their freedom.

We encamped in a beautiful valley which afforded an abundance of grass, on which our animals luxuriated after the bad fare of last night. In the afternoon, Lieut. Peck and I mounted our horses and started off to make an examination of the cañon. We were caught on the tongue of land which separates the forks of a tributary cañon, and at length found ourselves upon the brink of a stern precipice from 150 to 200 feet perpendicular, and on either side was an impassable ravine. These, uniting at our feet, swept onwards to join the river. Through the bottom a small stream of water pursued its meandering course, silent and slothful. The rocks on both sides were cut down vertically, so as to render it impossible to clamber down even afoot. The detritus, which the disintegrating action of the weather had accumulated, formed an immense talus, which was strewed with huge fragments that had been disengaged from the vertical walls at its summit. The rocks were highly ferruginous sandstone, rusty and blackened by oxidation, and harmonized well with the dark green foliage of the cedar.

As we gazed on the rude disorder, some buzzards, started from their perches by our intrusion, circled around as if amazed at beholding apparitions so unusual. Silence hung heavy around—so heavy that it seemed oppressive. Singling a bird which circled overhead, I fired, more intent on breaking the stillness than in directing my aim. The noise seemed deafening. At last the many echoes died away and all again was silent.

Fully satisfied with the wild scene, we mounted our horses and retraced our steps, and on our way procured seed of a beautiful purple convolvulus, Ipomœa leptophylla [morning glory]. Determined the position of our camp to be in latitude 35° 50′ 43″, longitude 104° 10′ 19″.

August 30th.—We saw today great numbers of wild horses, Equus caballus, which naturalists argue have originated from the stock introduced by the Spaniards. The Indians we met use them for riding, while others only pursue and take them for the meat which they afford, which is said to be well flavored and preferable to that of the antelope.

In our journey today we have been forced to bear strongly towards the east in order to avoid the deep gullies which in rainy weather serve to drain the elevated plain upon which we now found ourselves; for, on looking to the south we saw it suddenly break off, and the eye plunged into an ocean of mist floating over a prairie of indefinite extent far below, now and then pierced by the tops of seeming islands, whose summits, on a level with our feet, had once formed an integral portion of

1845

this plain. Here the river escapes from the jaws of the cañon, where the rocks are piled up to the height of 600 feet. Being everywhere covered with a dense growth of timber, they present very much the appearance of rising mountains, and were mistaken by Kendall, who approached them from below, on his expedition to Santa Fe, for the eastern spur of the Rocky Mountains.

The valley of the Canadian, 4[oo] or 500 feet below, lay spread out to the breadth of 12 or 15 miles, roughened by isolated ledges of rock and curiously shaped buttes, being bounded on the opposite side by cliffs scarcely discernible. It was in vain that we endeavoured to trace the meandering of the ravine, which was faintly marked by a few cottonwood trees that grew on its banks, as they were soon lost in the haze which hung like a mantle over the valley. We were much struck with the singular appearance of the lower strata of rocks, which here assumed a red or bright scarlet appearance. The crest of the bluff bounding the plain upon which we were now situated runs off in a direction slightly north of east for 12 or 15 miles; then, turning suddenly, bears northeast, and finally north as far as the eye can reach, so that all further progress is completely intercepted by a cliff from 4[oo] to 500 feet high.

Continuing our journey, and constantly forced by the nature of the country still further from the river, we reached a passable camping ground in the bottom of a small ravine and turned our animals out to graze, having made a march of 22 miles. We found here plenty of grapes and plums —the latter not yet fully ripe. This country abounds with timber, and on an elevated ground to the east of us is a fine grove of timber. Among the animals we noticed today were several land turtles, Cistudo clausa, which doubtless feed on a species of fungi which is often seen on the plains and resembles the common mushroom, except the lamellæ, which are colourless.

Sunday, August 31st.—As we found ourselves getting still further from the route we wished to pursue, and the way every hour becoming worse, it was resolved to attempt the descent. After traveling 1 ½ miles we found ourselves on the edge of the precipice which separated us from the plain below. After some search a point was discovered at which we thought it possible to descend. Whilst endeavouring to find a better route, my mule started down an inclination so abrupt that she commenced sliding along without power to stop. When we came to a place nearly two feet perpendicular, I held my breath as she shot over, and found myself seated on her neck, when, quickly turning her head uphill, I managed to dismount and replace the saddle. After a series of mishaps, among which the most serious was the breaking of my gunstock, I succeeded in reaching the bottom, and found Mr. Fitzpatrick, who had also preceded the caravan for the purpose, reconnoitring. Although he was not well satisfied with the route he had discovered, it would have been impossible to have brought them down by the route I had taken. Having cleared the loose fragments of rock from an inclined slope of 150 feet in length, which terminated in a shelf and from which we thought to find a winding path to the bottom, the mules were taken from the wagons, and by means of ropes they were let down one by one. With much labor, and after six hours, we had the satisfaction of seeing them safely landed on the plain below.

The day had been excessively warm and all were anxious to find water. We had seen cottonwoods to the eastward which from the crest of the cliff appeared about two miles distant, and near them we confidently expected to find water. Urged by extreme thirst we pressed hastily forward, panting for the water which seemed to flee before us; but the distance, instead of two miles, had grown to seven. There we found many pools lying along the course of a stream; but as the men alighted, with the joyful expectation of cooling their parched lips, they found the water too salt to drink.

We are now upon a vast alluvial plain extending indefinitely towards the east and composed of sand, small gravel, and angular fragments of rock. The cliff was underlaid with new red sandstone, of a color so remarkably bright that should a painter, in sketching the landscape, give it the true tone of color, he likely would be censured for exaggeration.

The stream we first struck was the Arroyo de los Yutas or, as the Comanches call it, Salt Creek. That which we finally encamped on was a tributary to it. The sandy plain over which we had just passed was strewed with numerous flowers, which indicated a change of soil. Blue, red, and yellow were common; the yellow, however, predominated—cacti, and the prairie sensitive plant, Schrankia angustata. We saw many new plants which had not been found on the northern prairies, and again had to regret our misfortune in not being able to save specimens. In the vicinity of our camp the sunflower, Helianthus, grew abundantly, and a species of belladonna, [family] Solanaceæ, which had passed the flowering season and was thickly covered with its round yellow seed balls. There were also several species of Convolvulus, amongst which was the Ipomœa leptophylla.

As we lazily smoked our pipes by the campfires that evening, we looked back upon the precipice which we had passed as the end of all our difficulties from rocks, and congratulated ourselves on our safe descent from the rugged heights which had so seriously annoyed Mr. Stanley's party just twenty years before. As far as we could discern, the lower strata of the ledge consisted of deep red sandstone, whilst the ground, of a like deep red color, was strewed with sand formed by the disintegration of both the brown and red sandstone.

Our astronomical observations gave us a latitude of 35° 41' 56.6" and longitude 103° 45' 05". Upon descending the cliff we noticed a variety of Gallinæ resembling the common quail, Perdix virginiana, with the exception of the crest. We supposed it to be P. californica, described by Audubon in his celebrated "American Ornithology," but we were unable to determine certainly, as they were with young, and their anxious care for the safety of their brood rendered them so shy as to defeat all our attempts to approach them.

September 1st.—Before we had proceeded far we found a rapid running stream, and all knelt down to take refreshing draughts. Sweet, indeed, was the water after the salt-flavored fluid which we had been obliged to drink last night. On leaving the camp we had taken a direction varying a little from southeast, with the intention of passing to the left of a distant butte which seemed to be the last of the rocky range and which formed the divide between the Arroyo de los Yutas and the Canadian; but as we advanced into the hills the traveling became extremely difficult on account of the continued occurrence of sand and cut rock, and we were glad to return to the valley of the Arroyo and content ourselves with following its windings. This stream, which last evening presented only pools of standing water, had here, from the accession of several small streams, and probably from springs rising out of the sand, become some yards in width, with rapid current, and where we crossed (16 miles below) had lost so much of the salt taste as to be palatable. The water was highly colored by the red sedimentary matter derived from the rocks and soil.

The valley, though sandy, appeared fertile, being covered with high grass and multitudes of yellow flowering plants. The numerous beautiful autumnal flowers we passed today recalled the idea of an immense flower garden and carried us back to the time when we first struck the Missouri prairies. Among the many varieties scattered around in wild profusion we observed the Adam's needle, Yucca angustifolia, the sensitive plant, Schrankia angustata, species of Convolvulaceæ, Leguminosæ, and Solaneæ. A grove of large cottonwood, surrounded by a natural meadow of fine tall grass, made our camp one of the best we had found, and as our animals were nibbling the choice food we took a stroll to a high butte 4 miles distant from which we obtained an extensive view of the neighboring country. Just below, the valley seemed barred by a transverse ridge through which the stream had cut a narrow gateway. To the south the beautiful valley of the Canadian spread out, covered with scattering buttes, amongst which we saw a band of mustangs. A heavy line of timber marked the course of the river itself, and we judged that we were still 12 miles distant from it, but were inexpressibly satisfied to find that it was now making northing.

The hill we had ascended differed in appearance from those we had been accustomed to see, having, instead of the abrupt ascent with sharp crest and flattened top, a gently rounded surface, and was covered with pebbles which bore evidence of the action of water as they were much rounded by attrition. With them we found a great intermixture of coarse gravel; it resembled in many respects the moraines so abundant in many parts of eastern Massachusetts.

In the neighborhood of the camp were quails, Perdix virginianus, whistling in the prairies. As we listened to the familiar note, "Bob White," it seemed as if some old friend would suddenly appear. We also whistled "Bob White" in hopes to lure him into view, for it was the first we had heard on our route since leaving Bent's Fort.

We experienced some difficulty in crossing the streams which intersected our trail. Although now dry, yet they are deep and the banks cut vertically by the immense bodies of water which rush through during the rainy season; for these little ravines carry off the drainage of a wide extent of prairie, whose surface, baked in the hot sun, absorbs but little of the water which the clouds sometimes so boisterously shower upon them. We found on the plain a specimen of Acacia commonly called "musquit" [mesquite], which the Indians manufacture into a farinaceous preparation similar to the "pinole" of the Spaniards.

September 2nd.—A few yards below our camp we crossed the stream by laying willow branches on the sand, which gave the bed of the stream sufficient solidity to bear the weight of our wagons. After a rough march of about five miles, we struck a faint trail, which we followed, and our scrutiny was rewarded by finding a piece of wood bearing evident marks of a knife. In addition to this, we had yesterday picked up a piece from a mass of float-wood bearing marks of an auger, indubitably the work of a white man; and [it] conveyed to us the pleasing intimation that we were in a country which had recently been traversed by civilized beings. It had no doubt been fashioned to supply some defective piece of a wagon, or carreta, for the rude workmanship and other marks led us to infer that it was the work of the Spanish "ciboleros," who are in the habit of making excursions into the eastern plains for the purpose of procuring supplies of buffalo meat, as well as of trading with the Indians. We drew another favorable inference from the rude fragment; which was, that we were on the most feasible road for descending the Canadian. We were aware that they could not have passed the grand cañon; they must, therefore, have come through [the] "Angosturas,"[23] passing the river below, and reached the stream on which we were by following the base of the bluff and crossing the spur which we had ascended to reconnoitre. We crossed the rocky barrier and descended to the plain below, where was the trail on which the wagons or carts had passed. Although faint, it could be distinguished by the color of the grass which grew upon it. This trail led us to a ledge which bordered the arroyo down which the Spaniards had passed. At the foot of the bluff we found what had been once a rude axletree. There was also a deep rut curving abruptly, which showed that they had locked the wheels for the purpose of descending the hill, when, the chain giving way, the cart had capsized, and the axletree got broken, and the scattered chips explained that it was there that it had been repaired. Had a civilized wheelwright seen the axle of one of these carretas, he would have been completely at a loss what to call it. Some persons say that the wheels are square and that the motion resembles the jumping of a grasshopper.

We are now in a shady grove of tall buttonwood, Platanus occidentalis, mingled with cottonwood. Whilst making preparations to ford the stream we found a few grapes, which proved extremely grateful. On our first approach, Hatcher had descried a band of wild horses and endeavoured to approach them that he might try the experiment of "creasing";[24] but they were aware of

---

23. Cf. Kendall, *Narrative* (1844), Vol. I, p. 261: "On either hand, the frowning and rocky sides of mountains rose high above us, and we now knew and felt that we were in the *Angosturas*, or Narrows of the river."

24. Cf. Gregg, *Commerce of the Prairies* (1844), Vol. II, chap. xi: "The mustang is sometimes taken by the cruel expedient of 'creasing,' which consists of shooting him through the upper crease of the neck, above the cervical vertebrae; . . . the wound heals without leaving any physical injury. But . . . many are killed in the attempt."

him, and we soon saw them emerge from the timber and gallop away over the wide-extended prairie. Ascending the bluff, the trail became more marked as it led over an elevated prairie covered with tall and wiry bunch grass; but finding it would carry us too far north, we left it and bore south. After descending 150 to 200 feet, we found ourselves in the bottom of the main river, just at the point where it is joined by the Arroyo de los Yutas.

A series of astronomical observations gave us, for this point, latitude 35° 20′ 59″, longitude 103° 29′ 38″ west of Greenwich.

Since we left the Canadian, at El Vado de Piedras [Rocky Ford], it has increased to 70 or 80 feet in width, with a deep and very rapid current, so that we could scarcely keep our feet whilst bathing. Its waters are colored, like its tributaries, and have thereby acquired the name of "Rio Colorado"[25] from the Spaniards and "Goo-al-pa" from the Indians. The name Canadian,[26] however, is retained as expressive of the nature of the channel through which it flows.

The bottom in which we encamped is everywhere covered with various species of cactus, the sharp spines of which penetrated our moccasins, making it painful to walk about. There is a plant still more annoying, commonly called "sandbur." This is a diminutive plant, lying close to the sandy surface, loaded with a profusion of little burs which attach themselves to our clothes and blankets by their sharp prickles and adhere with great tenacity. Amongst the sylva, the hackberry, Celtis crassifolia, is quite common, and we observed for the first time an extensive grove of the pride-of-India, Melia azedarach—a tree gifted with a beautiful form and dense foliage, not more than 30 feet in height, and covered with yellow fruit containing a single nut having a pulpy exterior, which was exceedingly disagreeable to the taste and so pungent that it was a long time before I could get rid of the unpleasant impression it produced. The trees were everywhere loaded with heavy masses of grapevines, Vitis æstivalis, which afforded the whole camp a great abundance of fruit. As we gathered the rich purple clusters, we thought they equalled in flavor any of the cultivated varieties. It was now the fruit season of the broad-leafed cactus, Opuntia, and they were everywhere in great abundance and of a size exceeding any we had hitherto met with, some being 3½ inches in length. In their flavor the raspberry and watermelon seemed mingled. They are sweet, cooling, highly mucilaginous, and filled with flat whitish seed, and considered preferable to the grapes. We frequently paid dearly for handling them, the little spines being barbed like a fishhook. We saw today great quantities of the "musquit," or "muskeet," covered with its long sabreformed legumes.

The creek is well timbered, but the high rocks conceal it until we reach the very verge. At this place is what is called the "Spanish Crossing," where the people of New Mexico pass with pack mules on their way to and from the Comanche country. Two deeply cut ruts gave to the trail the appearance of a wagon road, but their sometimes variable parallelism showed that they were formed principally by the feet of passing animals. We noticed a variety of cactus here, Cactus elatior; the joints were ovate and oblong, covered with exceedingly long spines. On opening several of the pericarps we found them defective, containing only six or eight small seed. This plant was very troublesome to our animals, for, when touched, the joints would fly off, adhere to the flesh, and cause much pain. The restiveness of the mules made it very difficult to remove these barbed spines, particularly as we were obliged to use the knife in order to save the fingers.

---

25. That is, Red River. There were a number of "Red" rivers in explorers' accounts and on maps. The redness of the water was especially remarked by men from less colorful regions. Cf. Latrobe, *The Rambler in North America* (1835), Vol. I, p. 184: "The Red Fork [the Cimarron] appeared worthy of its name, pouring down into the main river [the Arkansas] at our feet, a turbid bright red stream"; also p. 243: "Both the soil and the waters [between the Arkansas and the Canadian] were generally vermillion in color."

26. Abert's report printed as a Congressional Document reads thus. The Archives manuscript reads "Cañadian"; see note 22 above.

"Mis-Stan-stur — Cheyenne

September 3rd.—We commenced following the Goo-al-pa, meeting with scarcely any obstructions although the road was strewed with the broken axletrees of the Spanish carts which had preceded us. On the way we found quantities of luscious plums on the sand hills, although some wanted a little longer exposure to the ripening sun. We camped in the Canadian bottom again, near an old Spanish camp; there we found a few poles upon which some withered leaves still remained, showing they had been cut this season, and the pickets to which the animals had been attached were still standing.

Before reaching the river we again fell in with the trail which we had left yesterday and which we found bore to the north only for the purpose of cutting off a deep bend of the river.

7. Prairie Fire · Thunderstorm · Scenes of "Grand Sublimity"

Soon after our tents were pitched, a scene occurred which might have been attended with serious consequences and which threw us into momentary alarm. We were always obliged to burn a place in the prairie, in the centre of which the fire is built, some of the people standing by with blankets ready to prevent its spreading too far. In this instance the fire got beyond all control, but fortunately the wind was blowing from our camp and by much exertion the fire was kept from spreading in that direction. The tall reeds which grew so luxuriantly in the valley below us with a loud crackling noise were soon swept away by the devouring flame. Soon it reached the trees on the side of the bank and, leaping from bough to bough, quickly despoiled them of their verdant foliage; then, mounting the bluff, was borne rapidly off over the far-spreading prairie. About 7 o'clock in the evening it had extended to a great distance and was rapidly advancing in a semicircular form, the wind still blowing north 40° west.

The flames having disturbed the equilibrium of the atmosphere, a countercurrent soon bore back a heavy black cloud, composed of three lobes, which advanced until directly over our heads, when a severe thunderstorm broke upon us, illuminated by vivid flashes of lightning. In the evening we went to the top of the ridge which skirts our valley, the better to view this grand phenomenon. The sky overhead still shrouded with clouds, which glared with the bright red reflections, the strong black which the night threw around, and the vivid light of the fire, formed a "chiaro oscuro" which would have charmed a lover of Rembrandt. The crackling of consuming vegetation and the low murmurings of the whirling eddies of wind which skirted the burning edge deepened the impression of this scene of grand sublimity.

September 4th.—We left camp at half past 6 o'clock and traveled over the blackened prairie until half past 8 o'clock. We passed within a few feet of the flame without any apprehension. I think that individual risk has been much exaggerated; for, by waiting the near approach of the fire, one might easily spring through and reach the space over which the devastating element had already swept off all that was inflammable. Mr. Fitzpatrick observed that he had never yet seen the fire he could not escape by dashing quickly through the flames.

The trail led us through four or five miles of high and rounded sand hills wrought into regular form by the winds. The deep sand, yielding under the feet of the mules, made our progress slow and toilsome. The day was hot, and as we held our course over the barren waste without sign of water we languished and feared we should not find that necessary article. Our sufferings were greatly alleviated by the refreshing fruit of the plum tree, which everywhere grew in great abundance, and we found the fruit equal to any of the cultivated varieties that we recollected to have tasted in the United States.

At length we caught a glimpse of some tall cottonwoods. The sight of their green branches peeping over the sand buttes dispelled all our fears; for, in a little while after, we reached a beautiful valley where we found a clear cold spring, which of late had been an unusual occurrence. Our camp was formed under a grove of unusually tall cottonwoods, the characteristic sylva of this region, which heavily timbered the course of the rill which flowed from the spring. A few yards north of our camp were a few low buttes covered with dwarf plum trees profusely laden with fruit not perfectly ripe; as they grew in such luxuriant abundance, we plucked many branches and brought them to camp out of mere curiosity, when one of the messes made a useful appropriation of them by making a nondescript pudding which, had it not been for the fruit, one might liken to sailor's duff. They kindly sent some to our mess, and at that time we thought it excellent.

8. COMANCHE COUNTRY · FLOWERS OF THE PLAINS · UNSEEN INDIANS

We were now getting into a country where the utmost precaution became necessary to guard against the surprise or attack of the roving Comanches. A day or two previous we had seen the telegraphic signal fires, and the answering smoke, which conveyed the intelligence of strangers, and perhaps enemies, in the country, to the main band, which we supposed to be near. Mr. Fitzpatrick directed the enclosure of a "kraal," which we formed by felling large trees and arranging them in such a manner as to describe the arc of a circle, interlacing them with small branches, the remainder of the circle, completed by the wagons and tents, giving us a pretty strong position of defence which would enable us to make a successful resistance unless completely overwhelmed by numbers. These precautions were never afterwards neglected while traveling through the Comanche country, when we were able to find the necessary timber. When wood could not be found, we endeavoured to make such a selection for the position of our camp as afforded some natural obstruction, such as a deep ravine, a bluff bank, with which our wagons could be so disposed as to render abortive any attempt to charge through the camp, which is the most usual mode of attack.

The Spaniards appear to have cached their carretas at this place previous to their entering the Indian country, as the road here changes from a wagon trail to a bridle path. This idea was further confirmed by the appearance of a cart made in the rude style of the Spaniards of Mexico. Two eccentric wheels, not exactly circular, formed by sawing off the ends of large logs, and rimming them with pieces of timber to increase the diameter, presented an appearance not dissimilar to the wheels sometimes seen for crushing apples in a primitive cider press. They were perforated in the neighborhood of the centre to receive an axletree of cottonwood. A suitable pole and a little square box of wickerwork completed the laughable machine. The appearance of the identical cause unraveled to us the curious irregularities observed in the path and fully accounted for the numerous fragments we had noticed along the trail. We found here a great number of wild turkeys and a fine flock of ducks. On looking in the direction of our yesterday's camp, immense columns of smoke were seen still rolling upwards to the sky, and towards night the reddish glare caused some apprehension lest the fire should reach our camp.

September 5th.—We continued on the same trail as yesterday until about 8 o'clock, when, finding that we were rapidly diverging from the river, we were forced to leave it and to shape our course almost direct for the Goo-al-pa. We passed through a sandy country similar to that through which we traveled yesterday, and, after a toilsome march of 17 miles, reached the bank, cañoned by bluff escarpment 100 feet high and absolutely impossible of descent. We were obliged to make a retrograde movement, and camped in a deep tortuous ravine where we found a little stream of clear water, in which I had a delightful bath where it made a very abrupt bend back on itself and seemed enclosed by a coliseum of rocks. The valley appeared full of grapevines, and the troublesome sandburs covered the ground. In one of the crevices of the rocks we found a polecat, Mephitis americana. The French people who were with us caught it and ate it. The odor, however, was too pungent to suit everyone's olfactories.

We saw today an abundance of musquit, a species of Leguminosæ which has been thought by some persons to be the same as the Acacia arabica. It is a thorny shrub scarcely ever attaining the height of 5 feet. The legumes are long, sabre-form, cylindrical, and nearly white, filled with a solid substance of sweetish taste from which the Comanches and Kioways manufacture a kind of flour. Gregg states that in some of the fertile valleys of Chihuahua it attains the height of 30 and 40 feet, with a trunk from 1 to 2 feet in diameter. We saw here an abundance of the cardinal flower, Lobelia cardinalis. They looked most brilliantly as they glistened in bright scarlet array among the green plants which grew so luxuriantly along the border of the stream as to conceal it in many places entirely.

The rocks around were of limestone underlaid with new red sandstone. On the top of the bluffs just above our heads we found some huge petrified logs in which the ligneous matter had been replaced by some ferruginous composition, which, by long exposure to the wind and rain, had become so completely oxidized that had it not been for their peculiar shape they might have been mistaken for large pieces of iron ore.

Antelopes are abundant, and, as usual, the prairie is covered with shore larks, Alauda alpestris, the Alauda cornuta of Swainson.[27] We saw them in abundance on the plains during the whole of our journey. These little birds are found during the winter season on the commons about the city of Washington. We also found the cacti, Argemone mexicana [prickly poppy], and yucca, of the plains; the Populus canadensis [cottonwood] and Arundo canadensis [giant reed], near the streams; and in the ponds we found the Typha latifolia [cattail], Nymphæa lutea [yellow water-lily], and Sagittaria sagittifolia [arrowhead].

September 6th.—After quite a pleasant march on the level prairie, we attempted to reach the river, and, knowing that there were high banks which coasted it, we undertook to reach its valley by the way of a tributary ravine, and after a terribly rough pull over rugged hills and dales we were glad to avail ourselves of the buffalo paths in order to extricate the party from this difficult pass. Many of the wagon mules had entirely given out and were replaced by animals from the cavalcade, and before reaching camp we had the misfortune to break the tongue of one of the wagons.

We were made a little uneasy today by the discovery of an Indian trail the breadth and freshness of which showed that Indians were near and in great numbers. Tonight we made our beds under the canopy of the starry heavens, which shone so luminously that there was more pleasure in tracing the various constellations than in endeavouring to sleep. Everyone must be struck with the extraordinary brightness of a prairie sky, due to the singular purity of the atmosphere. This property of the atmosphere is also exemplified by the manner in which meat can be cured, merely by drying it in the sun, and by the absence of dews.

Among the plants which were most abundant we noticed the artemisia and the Cucurbita aurantia, which are characteristic of the plains since leaving Bent's Fort. We also found overgrowing the dry ponds or buffalo wallows the Myrtinia proboscidea [unicorn plant]. St. Pierre describes it[28] as peculiar to Vera Cruz [and] attributes to it traits so singular that we could not notice the plant without relating them. He says: "I presume that often when the shores of Vera Cruz are overflowed by high tides you must see fishes caught by this plant, for the stem of its pod is not easily broken off; its two crotchets, pointed like fishing hooks, are elastic and hard as horn. Besides, when it is soaked in water, its furrows, shaded with black, shine as if they were filled with globules of quicksilver. Now, the lustre of this light is a further bait to attract the fishes." Horned lizards, Agama cornuta, are also in abundance, and increased in number as we proceeded. Dr. Harlan describes a

27. Cf. William Swainson in *The Philosophical Magazine*, ser. 2, Vol. I (1827), p. 434: "To continue the specific name of *Alpestris* to a bird which, as Wilson affirms, is seen only upon sandy plains, is a manifest absurdity. I have therefore adopted the alteration which that accurate observer himself has suggested."

28. Cf. Bernardin de Saint-Pierre on "the martinia" in the 1807 English edition of his *Works*, Vol. III, pp. 92–93.

second variety, which is called the Agama Douglassii, but confines its habitation to the plains of the Oregon or Columbian River.[29] Although we did not bring specimens all the way with us, we noticed many with the horns not well developed, and since we have had an opportunity of comparing the two agamas, have concluded that the A. Douglassii inhabit the region through which we are now passing.

We find the Canadian still increasing in width and velocity of its waters, which have now a deep tinge and justly merit the name of "colorado."

A fine series of observations gave us a latitude of 35° 31′ 36″ and longitude 102° 47′ 02″ west of Greenwich.

Sunday, September 7th.—Camp 25. Before we had proceeded far, we struck into an Indian trail and saw from the freshness of the track that a party had recently passed. As the trail leaves the river here, and bears towards the divide, we congratulated ourselves that by leaving it for the bank of the river we had missed their village, which we were not particularly anxious to see at that time.

The Indians are remarkable for the skill displayed in the selection of their trails, which are always the most practicable routes through the country; but as they have no wagons to incumber them, we were sometimes led into difficulties which required the constant exercise of our ingenuity to overcome; nevertheless, we clung closely to the trail, as it at least afforded an excellent guide to the best wagon road. We followed on and found the bluffs leveling and the traveling improving. A few miles brought us to the site of an old Indian camp. We noticed peculiarities which showed that it belonged to a different tribe from those we had hitherto been acquainted with. The singular ring with stones heaped in the centre marked the site of the "medicine lodge"; also, showed that it had been occupied by the Comanches. As there were few traces of lodges having been used, but principally rude wigwams, Hatcher pronounced that they had belonged to the Buffalo Eaters, one of the most ferocious bands of the Comanche nation. This band follow the migratory herds of buffaloes, eat their flesh, and clothe themselves in their skins. The discovery of this encampment led us to suppose that their favorite game must be at hand, and in this we were confirmed by seeing tracks of buffaloes in the sand a little further on. Crossing a stream, we found under some cottonwoods close to the margin of the river the still warm embers of their fires, which, with the fresh track in the moist sandy bed of the river, induced us to believe that they had rested here last night.

While we were carefully examining the spot our attention was suddenly riveted by a remarkable sound resembling the cry of some animal in great distress. On searching for the cause we found a large black snake which had caught a poor frog by the foot, whose perilous situation had caused the cry which attracted our attention. We wished to see how the snake would manage to gulp him down, but Hatcher, drawing his scalping knife before anyone could speak, had decapitated the serpent, and the frog, finding himself at liberty, immediately leaped into the water.

The sandy bed of the river is here 100 yards wide; the water, dwindled to a small stream by the absorbing material through which it flows, is slowly meandering, and as we travel on is alternately rising and disappearing. After a march of 19 miles we again formed our kraal in the bottom; but no sooner were our tents pitched than we were attacked by myriads of musketoes, which not only drove sleep from our eyes but the idea of it from our heads.

Our road today was everywhere beautified by a luxuriant profusion of plum trees and grapevines, and our disappointment was great on finding the fruit had been taken by the Indians who had recently passed. The trail through the deep sand was still marked with strong impressions of the feet of their mules and horses. In the neighborhood of our camp we found several coveys of quails. One of them having alighted on the tall cottonwood, we requested Hatcher to try his skill with the rifle. On the report of the gun the bird fell to the ground with its head severed from the body.

29. Cf. Harlan, *Medical and Physical Researches* (1835), pp. 141–142.

Nah-cot-se-west.
Brother of "Mis stan Star".

Not having met with game, we killed an ox today, which proved to be very fat and afforded us the enjoyment which can only be experienced by those who have been encamped on a desolate desert. Here every little comfort becomes magnified when contrasted with the inhospitality which surrounds us, and increases the satisfaction of the triumphs achieved over the difficulties and obstacles which such a situation produces. Great is the pleasure we enjoy when [we are] assembled around the laughing flames of a warm fire and see the choice pieces of meat hissing before it, with appetites excited by the wholesome exercise of our march and stimulated by the savoury incense which arises from the smoking viands.

September 8th.—We still continued to follow the Indian trail, which we find of the greatest assistance in traveling over these trackless wilds; although it sometimes lay along the bottom and sometimes ascended the bluff, yet always affording a good guide to the best route.

In the morning an Indian showed himself on the hills who appeared to be a scout. He continued to travel abreast of us for half an hour and always at a respectful distance. He resisted all invitations to join us, and even refused to meet a single horseman sent from our party. Having satisfied himself, he turned over the hill and galloped away. The apparition of this strange character convinced us that there was a party near, and kept those disposed to straggle very close to the main body during the remainder of the march.

About noon we found a stream of delightful cool water, which ran swiftly along the bottom of a deep-cut ravine completely shaded from the sultry sun by the luxuriant growth of grass and reeds which overtopped the backs of our mules. We frequently stopped and drank of the pure stream as we followed it to its source in order to head it, as we could not cross without great difficulty.

Shortly after, we saw two large patches of ground covered with a seeming coralline formation, whereupon Lieut. Peck and myself dismounted to procure specimens. We found the madrepore structure wanting, and concluded, from its peculiar friability and composition, that it must be a siliceous deposit of some extinct thermal spring.

9. Buffalo Chase · Encounter with a Wolf · Comanches: Buffalo Eaters

We were now slowly advancing up the long slope of a sandy hill, when, peeping over the ridge, we saw a deep ravine the bottom of which was covered with buffaloes. We all silently drew up in a line along the crest of the bluff, that we might obtain a view of the first band of buffaloes we had seen on the Canadian. Some were quietly feeding on the nutritious vegetation; others lazily reclining on the tender grass, chewing the cud; here and there clouds of dust ascending, from the midst of which the hollow bellowing of bulls was heard, dashing at each other in dread combat. Whilst [we were] regaling our eyes with this glad sight, an old voyageur was despatched in the anticipation of luxuriating on the fat ribs and tender loins; but some of the animals perceiving him, the alarm was instantly given throughout the band, and we saw them all gallop away and disappear behind the hills. We were not, however, doomed to be disappointed, for, before concluding our march, Hatcher came in with [the meat of] a fine fat cow thrown across his mule. Having showed him where we should encamp, he again sallied forth, and soon returned with three mules laden with the meat of four buffaloes which he had killed from the same herd.

When a hunter succeeds in approaching a herd undiscovered, he can often kill as many as ten or fifteen without "raising" the band. They pay very little attention to their fallen companions unless an unsuccessful shot strikes and wounds one that communicates his fright to the rest of the band. The bulls and calves are scarcely ever used. The former are sometimes killed in the spring, but at all other seasons their flesh is said to be rank and unpleasant. In shooting the cows the hunter always selects the fattest in the band. In butchering them the skin is cut open on the back and the meat on each side of the long spines of the vertebral column, termed the "fleece," is then removed, and the spines themselves, broken off close to the vertebræ, form that part called the "hump ribs," a favorite part; then comes the "bass," just back of the neck, the side ribs, and tongue. The remainder is generally left to the wolves. Sometimes the large bones of the legs are brought in for the marrow, which, when roasted, is delicious, much resembling butter and of a deep yellow color.

This animal is termed by most writers the "Bos americanus" and is said to be indigenous. They are generally of a dark-brown color, although some have been seen almost white; yet such may be considered anomalies, and are so very rare that Mr. Fitzpatrick tells me that during his long residence of upwards of twenty years in this country he had seen only two or three. The hair about the head and beard is very long, gradually diminishing to the furthest edge of the scapula, where it changes to the usual length of that of the common ox. The tail is very short, reaching only to the houghs, and is tufted. In running, and when the animal is excited, its tail is erected as a banner of defiance. The underside of the forearm is heavily clad with long hair, giving a singular appearance to the animal when in motion. The cow is smaller, and her hair more uniform in length, as well as the diameter of the horn, which in the bull varies [*changed in manuscript from* increases] rapidly. By this the sexes are easily distinguished, even by a glance at the skull, many of which we examined and sketched. The eye is remarkably round, and gifted with great mobility; becomes enlarged and inflamed when the animal is enraged, and possesses at such times a look of indescribable fierceness.

One afternoon when on a buffalo chase, being separated from my companions, I was returning to camp when my attention was attracted to a large bull which had been wounded in the spine, and his hind legs were trailing on the ground. Having succeeded in approaching him, when quite near, he turned, and such was the ferocity depicted on his front that my horse (which in the excitement of the chase had borne me unhesitatingly through the midst of the herd) now seemed perfectly appalled, and quailed beneath the fiery glance of the infuriated animal. I plied my spurs in vain, for my horse commenced to retrograde with his eye firmly fixed on the object of terror. Yielding to his fears, I was slowly wending my way towards camp when a large wolf, Canis lupus, started from his skulking place with a hissing sound, then trotted off a short distance and stopped to gaze at me. He appeared old, gaunt, and mangy, with arched back bristling like a hyena; looked the picture of ravenous ferocity. At the report of my pistol he fled—doubtless he was on the watch for the wounded buffalo, as they always hang around the bands to attack the infirm and wounded, or to devour what the hunters leave.

The buffalo almost invariably moves in a gallop, when the long hair on the forearm flutters about like a pair of sailor's trowsers. The longer spinous processes of the anterior dorsal vertebræ, consisting of the hump ribs, measure from 1½ to 2 feet in length. These animals were observed in the Carolinas soon after the arrival of the first colonists, and also in Pennsylvania. They also existed wild in the State of Kentucky as late as the year 1766.

We pitched our tents at night on a point lying between the river and the bluff, which here comes to the water's edge, the third side of our camp being open. We had now plenty of good meat, and the utmost hilarity prevailed throughout the encampment notwithstanding a drizzling rain which commenced just at nightfall. Shortly before meeting with the buffaloes, we noticed a singular rock on the ledge of the opposite bank that might be useful as a landmark to future travelers.

September 9th.—The rain still continuing at intervals, we remained in camp all day to "make meat," which is done by cutting it in thin slices and putting it on scaffolds over the fire to dry, when it is packed in bales formed of hard dressed leather called parflèche.

For several days previous we had seen tracks of Indians so perfectly fresh that it seemed as if some invisible being had made them while we were but a short distance from the spot; still, but one Indian had been seen. Yesterday, when we first arrived, we noticed fresh tracks deeply impressed upon the sandy bottom of the river, where plum stones had been scattered around and several meat bones newly gnawed. Some of the men, while hunting, came suddenly upon one who evidently had approached in order to spy out the arrangement of our camp. They made signs in order to induce him to accompany them, but he secreted himself, and they, not knowing how many might be near, quickly returned to camp. In the afternoon a few Indians showed themselves on the top of the hill which commanded the open side of our camp. For a time they refused all our invitations to visit us; but on [our] displaying a white flag they ventured into the valley, where Mr. Fitzpatrick met them and succeeded in inducing them to accompany him into camp, when we found them to be a band of the Buffalo Eaters. Their fears once dispelled, they became quite familiar and examined our equipments and wagons with childlike interest.

Wishing to conciliate them, we gave them as much as possible, setting before them such eatables as our camp afforded, and presented them with some tobacco. They ate voraciously, and tasted the coffee which was prepared for them, but did not appear to relish it. We noticed one who, before raising the cup to his lips, dipped his forefinger in the cup and crossed himself in imitation of what he had seen done by the Spaniards,[30] with whom they hold some intercourse. They asked for paint for their squaws, which we were obliged to deny them, for this essential article in Indian negotiations formed no part of our outfit. They appeared dirty and mean—were badly dressed, but had fine horses, which must have been obtained in the incursions upon the traders of New Mexico, as was evident from their bridles and saddles, which were of Spanish make. [We] having explained to them the nation to which we belonged and the peaceable nature of our mission, they expressed their satisfaction and, mounting their horses, rode off to rejoin their village.

The river had been rising gradually during the day. On hearing a rush of water and looking out, we saw a foaming torrent bearing rapidly along with it trunks and branches of trees, and [it] appeared as if it had been pent up by a barrier which, suddenly yielding to accumulating pressure, had permitted the stream to rush forth. The river immediately doubled in depth and velocity and for a moment threatened to deluge our camp and at once dissipate our hope of being able to cross it and pursue our journey on the opposite side. We were therefore forced to clear a way along the base of the bluff. The men fell to work in good earnest and the road was completed for the wagons before night. The bottom here is pretty wide and bears marks of fertility, and is walled up by bluffs 100 feet high. These render the traveling difficult, as the river continually approaches close to their bases, so that it is necessary to ascend and descend the steeps every half mile.

We have the wild turkey in abundance in the neighborhood of our camp, and as they persisted in retaining possession of their accustomed roosts our men had a fine opportunity of trying their skill in shooting them.

September 10th.—At an early hour in the morning we were on our way and, soon leaving the bottom, entered a more desolate country than we had hitherto seen. The high and dry tablelands were covered with but a few scattered plants and were altogether desert-like.

The cacti and musquit were most abundant. In one place we noticed a quantity of the long pods of the last-mentioned plant which had evidently been thrown there by human hands. Whilst riding over a sandy waste we noticed a most delicious fragrance, which was to us, traveling on this wild desert, more sweet than blossoming orange groves or eastern bowers of roses such as perfume the famed Valley of Cashmere. All this sweetness arose from an unattractive little aster, a species of [the] Compositæ, which, growing in the barren sand, seemed intended to counteract by pleasant sensations the disagreeable effect of the burning reflections produced by the soil upon which it grew.

We followed the Indian trail with difficulty, for it was now and then entirely lost, as if they had

---

30. It was customary with them, as Catholics, to make a sign of the cross when saying grace before meals.

purposely endeavoured to prevent our following their route. Wherever we approached the river, we found it swollen and muddy, with a very rapid current.

From the idea impressed by the barrenness of the country it appeared incredible that so many Indians could obtain their subsistence from it.

The Indians have been following us all day but have not ventured into camp. They appear suspicious as to our designs and cannot be made to understand our object in traveling. They were told that it was neither to trade nor make war, which sorely puzzled them; for they could not conceive that any other objects would have brought men so far from their homes.

Buffaloes have not been seen today, having probably been frightened away by the neighboring Indians. We must except one old bull, which we noticed not far from our route, standing regardless of our approach. Hatcher went out and shot him and found that he had received a terrible wound in one of those terrific combats in which the bulls so often indulge. He had left the herd to die alone, for his wound would have proved mortal, and the death he owed to us only put an end to prolonged suffering.

We again found an abundance of prickly pears, grapevines, and plum trees. The Indians had plucked all the fruit except here and there a few bunches of grapes, which we found to be remarkably sweet. Our day's march was upwards of 27 miles, and the route so sandy that our mules were exceedingly harassed. We encamped close to the riverbanks, which were not more than 5 feet high, with the bottom extending back 300 feet to the base of the bluffs. Upon going into the river to bathe, I found the depth to be 2 feet, the current rapid, and so muddy that I durst not immerse myself in its waters, which were of a deep red color, and which obliged us to get our drinking water from the opposite side of the river. François Latulippe was here struck at by a very large rattlesnake, and one of our party, to revenge the act, took his pistol and, loading it with powder only, shot the venomous reptile in the mouth, holding the snake down by the means of a forked stick which he placed directly back of its head, when, thinking it sufficiently punished, he threw the serpent into the river, where for a while it struggled with the current but at length disappeared beneath its turbid waters.

We this morning obtained a fine specimen of the cranium of an Indian, but as all the most experienced of our voyageurs feared that it might be found in our possession we cast it into the river. It had been found by Lieut. Peck among some bones which had been arranged around it with great care. Nothing outrages the superstitious notions of the Indians so much as the disturbing of the bones of their dead. Hatcher told me that he had delighted them by taking some bones which the Spaniards had disinterred, painting them with vermilion, and wrapping them in cloth and burying them. Often, since, they had mentioned this act with grateful satisfaction.

The latitude, as determined by observation, was 35° 27′ 25″, longitude 102° 00′ 06″.

September 11th.—At 7 o'clock we found ourselves on our journey, but experienced some trouble by meeting continually with cut rock and deep ravines. Passing into a valley, beautiful in the freshness of its vegetation, we entered a bottom where the tall grass grew abundantly. As we wound along under a romantic cliff, we hoped to find better traveling, when our progress was suddenly stayed by a projecting bluff which rendered further advance impossible. To cross was impracticable; to recede would occupy too long a time; it was therefore resolved to attempt to ascend the bluff, which was here very steep and high. As we were preparing to do so, we were startled by the report of firearms, and, on looking in the direction from whence the sound proceeded, we discovered on the opposite side of the river a party of Indians perched upon the high rocky bluff, endeavouring to attract our attention. We motioned to them to advance, at the same time choosing our position so as to be flanked by the river on one side and a semicircular barrier of our wagons on the other. Into this kraal we were securely placed whilst waiting the approach of friend or foe.

Oka wo cum
White Antelope

Cheyenne — (no Eyebrows)
Sunday July 27th 1845

21

"Oco-chie-tah-nahun"
"Little Crow"
A Cheyenne —

Isse wo ne max ist
a
Cheyenne —

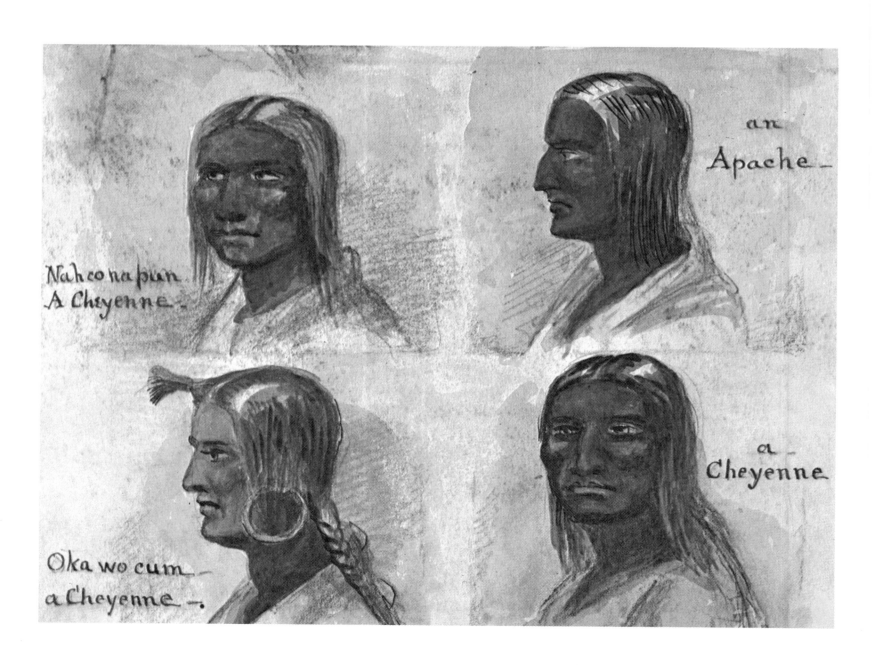

Nah co na pun
A Cheyenne —

an
Apache —

Oka wo cum
a Cheyenne —

a
Cheyenne

Little Mountain
a Kioway Indian
Thursday Sept. 18th
1845

Tah kai Buhl
A Kioway.

Shonka mah toh
A Sioux —
8th aug.
(4 Scalp locks.)

"Shaw me no"
A Delaware

Isse wo ne am in
august 7th
A Cheyenne —

They went some distance up the stream to obtain a practicable fording place, and we observed one of them carrying a little flag. Meeting them a short distance from the main body, we sat down and were soon deeply engaged in all the mysteries of Indian diplomacy. We learned that they belonged to the band of Buffalo Eaters and had been watching our movements. Seeing us about to leave the course of the river, they had now come to hold a talk and get some tobacco. They said that they had heard of our approach, and were not afraid; that most of their braves had gone, in company with the Kioways, to fight the Spaniards, and that they intended to overrun the lower country as far as Chihuahua.

The most agreeable news we received was that the Pawnees, who for a long time had been at war with the Comanches, had at length agreed to make peace, and that a few days before they had met, and were encamped quite near to each other, but on awaking in the morning they found their Pawnee friends had decamped and a great number of their horses had disappeared; upon which, they instantly started in pursuit and, after following their trail a long way, overtook them, recovered their horses without losing a single man, and succeeded in obtaining the scalp of one of their treacherous allies. They said that the "pong, pong, pong" of the war drum was still resounding through the hills and their hearts were all made glad by their successful retaliation. There was now no danger of our meeting with these rascally Indians. In return we communicated all we had heard which was likely to interest them. We noticed a Spaniard among them who was dressed in the Indian costume and appeared perfectly at ease although he had been taken prisoner in one of the depredatory excursions into the Mexican territory. His captors treated him very kindly and made a fair partition of the tobacco which we presented to them. In return they showed us a winding way to the top of the bluff. It was their lodge trail but proved impassable for wagons.

While searching for a practicable outlet we stopped near a large grove of hackberry, Celtis crassifolia, and gathered quantities of the berries, which, although not larger than a pea, and containing large seed, repaid us for our trouble by the pleasantness of their flavour, which resembles that of tea. We proceeded, following a wild ravine, but were obliged at last to force our wagons up a frightful steep by main strength, and then we reached the plain above.

10. Petrified Trees · Plain Strewed with Rose-and-blue Striped Agates

We noticed several trees in a state of petrifaction which were covered with sparkling masses of clear rock crystal, and the ligneous fibre had in some places been supplied by pink-colored agate, which, shining through, gave to the whole a brilliant rosy hue resembling rose quartz. The sides of the hills were covered with quartz in fragments and an abundance of coarse agates. On the top of the buttes we saw a ring of small stones, about 3 feet in diameter, which doubtless marks the last resting place of some individual of note.

Passing onward, the road for a time promised to be smooth, when suddenly an immense ravine yawned before us and we were on the brink of the river again, at a point where it was joined by one of its tributaries. As we looked onward, nothing but red precipices met our view, and they were piled up 250 feet perpendicular and perfectly impassable. We were fairly pocketed. On looking down into the deep cañon, instead of the beautiful green strip at the bottom, which we had hitherto seen, we discovered that it was covered with sand hills, red like the precipices that bound them, and the eye wanders over them wearied by the search for any resting-spot of green vegetation.

We now found ourselves obliged to turn back in order to head the ravine we had encountered. By continually recurring ravines we soon found ourselves in the vicinity of our starting point, and encamped on a neck of land between two valleys and at the head of a cañoned ravine, where there was a little standing water and a small quantity of grass for our animals. Our last half day's travel led us over a plain strewed with agates colored with stripes of rose and blue and with colors resulting from their admixture. They were coarse and of little value, but so numerous that we gave the place the name of Agate Bluffs.

11. Night Alarm · "Merry Meeting" with Friendly Kioways and Crows

September 12th.—Last night we were startled at midnight by the alarm of Indians. They had been heard early in the evening as they followed in our path, and an occasional dark form was seen flitting across the hill and disappearing in the cañon below. The mules, which are the best sentinels, were very restless, snorting, and some broke the tugs by which they were attached to the pickets, showing by their actions that a concealed enemy was prowling around. Just as the moon was setting, Hatcher, awakened by the unusual stir, got up and, taking his rifle, sat himself beside the door of our tent. Upon first hearing the alarm we all sprang to our feet, rifle in hand, but as no hostile demonstration succeeded we again returned to rest, having first examined the fastenings of our mules and taken every precaution to guard against surprise.

At daylight we were stirring and, on examining the neighborhood, found the tracks of Indians, and soon discovered a band of natives riding towards our camp. We invited them in and gave them breakfast, of which they partook with great confidence. They proved to be a band of Kioways, and several of the "Up-sah-ro-kees," or Crows, who live on the headwaters of the Missouri. They said that their village was on a branch of the creek upon which we were encamped. They, discovering our trail, which indicated the presence of strangers, had followed on until warned to proceed more cautiously by the alarm given in the early part of the evening. We had been mistaken by them for their enemies the Texans, and they had remained near our camp during the night in order to satisfy themselves.

One of them had crawled in the shadow of the ravine to within ten feet of our tent, where he lay quietly, entirely screened from observation by a rocky wall which ran perpendicularly down into the ravine. From this point he saw Hatcher and closely observed every motion: his rising in bed on his elbow, rolling up his sleeves, scratching his arm, and taking his rifle and seating himself at the door of the tent. Determined to improve so fine an opportunity of revenging himself on one whom he considered as an enemy, he fitted his arrow to the bowstring and drew it to the head; but, he added, "Here my heart whispered to me that he might be an American, and I did not shoot." This was indeed a dread moment—the lives of our whole party hung upon the Indian's bowstring. We were just entering their country; they were around us in numbers, and had blood been shed they would have hung about us until every individual was cut off; but the hand of Almighty Providence prevented this sad termination. The Great Spirit whispered in the ear of the savage, "He may be an American." To confirm his statement to us, as well as to prove to his brother warriors the boldness of his daring approach, he had piled a heap of stones on the ledge of the rock after yielding to the fortunate suggestion of his heart. We were also approached on the opposite side of our camp by several who had crept upon their bellies and watched the men sleeping under the wagons, and said that they could have stabbed them to the heart and retreated without being discovered.

Our camp was well chosen to resist any attack, being protected on two sides by deep ravines, whose rock-bound sides cut perpendicularly, which, although of great advantage against a charge, yet served to screen anyone who might endeavour to crawl up. Mr. Fitzpatrick had told the guard that the Indians might approach by this ravine, and one who had had long experience on the prairies had been charged to watch it particularly; yet, notwithstanding this caution and the warning given by the mules, the Indians, by their cunning, were enabled to elude all our precautions. The man who had so narrowly escaped was a trader to the nation to which the Indians belonged, and by daylight they recognised each other and heartily shook hands.

We were all delighted to find our "stern alarms" changed to a "merry meeting." We gave our new friends some tobacco and expressed our regrets at having nothing else to offer them. Hatcher made them some "segaritos"; they smoked them with seeming satisfaction and then mounted their horses and accompanied us on our road, which led us nigh their camp; they laughed heartily at a party of Comanches they had previously met, who had been frightened at our approach and fled, leaving their mules and furniture scattered over the prairie, and, meeting these Kioways, advised them to fly, as they reported us to be as numerous as the blades of grass on the prairie. These, however, were determined to satisfy themselves and, striking on our trail, had followed until last evening.

The Kioways are a people excelling the Comanches in every respect, and, though far inferior to them in number, not counting more than 200 lodges in all, yet exercise almost absolute control over them. On [our] inquiring the origin of their nation and the cause of their having such influence, they replied that many years ago, so long as to be lost to the memory of their oldest tradition, their fathers had left a land far to the north and, coming hither and finding the Comanches, had smoked the pipe of peace and had remained in close friendship ever since. They speak an entirely different language, being much more deep and guttural, striking upon the ear like the sound of falling water. Their manners and customs are also quite different, yet they are firmly bound together by some unseen bond and appear to feel a mutual desire to benefit each other. The Kioways sustain a character for bravery, energy, and honesty, while the Comanches are directly opposite, being cowardly, indolent, and treacherous.[31] The Kioways are particularly noted for their honesty, and while we remained with them nothing was stolen—an occurrence sufficiently uncommon to merit special notice.

Arrived at their village, we found it in a well-wooded valley embosomed by high hills. Their horses had eaten the grass very short; therefore ours found but indifferent pasturage. We encamped a quarter of a mile lower down, and had scarcely pitched our tents before the squaws and children came flocking round anxious to trade, some bringing ropes made of plaited thongs, some moccasins, and others skins. We had nothing but tobacco to offer them in exchange, and with this single article we effected a few purchases—for had we refused to trade altogether they would have imputed it to an unfriendly motive. We wished to conciliate them as much as possible, hoping to derive some benefit from them during our passage through the Indian settlements below, which they represented to be very numerous.

We were much struck by the noble bearing and fine athletic figures of these people, which we partly attributed to their being continually on horseback, which not only gives them palpable evidence of their superiority over the animals they bestride, but makes them conscious of their elevation over all the lower orders of creation, which is communicated to their whole character. The Indian, on the wide prairie, casts his eye around him and sees the wild horse, one of God's noblest gifts, skimming across the desert with the celerity of an arrow, and a new pride is awakened in his bosom when he reflects that this beautiful creature, so strong, so fleet, is subject to his power. These Indians ride beautifully and manage their horses with astonishing skill. Knowing their fondness for large American horses, I endeavoured to exchange mine, which, although it had been led all the way from Bent's Fort, was very stiff, but the chief said he had "two hearts" about it. We noticed the singularity of their mode of mounting: wrapping a blanket several times around their body and legs, they throw themselves lengthwise upon the horse, and then rise up in the seat. The blanket, binding the limbs, assists greatly in clinging to the animal.

These people, contrary to the general opinion, appeared to be gay, cheerful, and fond of frolic; they laughed, chatted, and joked, much to the astonishment of some of us, who possessed precon-

31. Hodge's *Handbook*, Vol. I, p. 327, says, to the contrary, that the Comanches "bore a reputation for dash and courage."

ceived notions which were, doubtless, obtained from the popular writers of the day. We noticed that they had learned from some wandering trader or hunter the peculiar gyratory motion of the hand which we sometimes find interpreted into the phrase "You can't come it." Some of the men had formed a shooting match between the boys, and they spent an hour or two in shooting at a button at the distance of 15 or 20 paces. We were all surprised at the remarkable skill which they displayed.

Among the people who came to visit us in the camp were some whose features and hair betokened Spanish blood; they had been taken prisoner, and, being well treated, were perfectly content with their new situation; they said that they were in fact better situated than in their own country, for they had plenty to eat and were more kindly treated than in the place whence they had been taken.

In dress the Kioways resemble the other roving tribes of the great desert, being habited in buckskin. Their moccasins are furnished with a fringed appendage 8 or 10 inches in length, which is attached to the heel, which could not be conveniently worn by other than mounted Indians and is said to be peculiar to their tribe. They all have the blanket or buffalo robe, and their long hair is braided so as to form a queue, sometimes lengthened by means of horsehair until it reaches the ground; and this queue is often ornamented with convex silver plates, which they procure from the Spaniards. The dress of the women differs but little from that of the northern tribes—the same leathern cape, tunic, leggins, and beaded moccasins. We were particularly struck with the profusion of trappings with which the men ornamented themselves and their horses, and which they had procured either by robbery or barter from the Spaniards, with whom they had considerable intercourse.

After finishing our trade, we endeavoured to persuade some of the Indians to travel with us, for we apprehended difficulties in coming into collision with some roving band that might attack us by night under the idea that we were Texans. There was one young man whose frank and generous demeanour elicited the sympathies and procured the friendship of all of us, and he too seemed at once to have his whole heart enlisted in our behalf. We endeavoured to persuade him to accompany us as far as Bent's [trading] houses, where we would perhaps meet a large assemblage of Indians awaiting the arrival of Bent's wagons. We told him at once that we had nothing to give him and therefore could not press him to incommode himself. He appeared undecided and returned to the village to consult the chiefs.

We were struck with the affection which an old squaw manifested for Hatcher. She wept over him for joy when they met, and insisted on his receiving a bale of tongues and some pinole which she had manufactured from the musquit. She always calls him son, having adopted him ever since his first trading with her nation.

At our last evening's camp we found beautiful masses of prismatic crystals of limpid quartz, the edges unabraded by attrition and glistening with the brilliancy of the diamond. These, with some agates, were shown to the Indians, who appeared to be well acquainted with their property of striking fire, and call the principal stream in the vicinity "Flint River."

September 13th.—This morning we had a serious debate as to the expediency of taking our wagons further or abandoning them to the Indians. They are a source of continued delay and vexation, and the way has presented new difficulties each day, for, being obliged to keep near the river, we are necessitated to pass over the roughest routes. We are also straitened for means to manufacture packsaddles, having neither hammer, nails, nor saw; we therefore concluded to try them three days longer, hoping that our poor animals, now worn out by hard fare and harder labour, might soon meet with better pasturage.

Shortly before reaching camp we were obliged to cross the bottom of a creek several times, and as the wheels sunk deep in the sand our mules suffered extremely. We had scarcely pitched our tents when we saw two braves and a squaw coming to join us, which they would have done before, but they had waited to paint themselves. They said that two Comanches had come up from below with a report that the Texans were coming to fight them and that they were persuaded by their chiefs to go with us in order to help us out of our difficulties. We received them cordially and assigned them a place for their wigwam. The principal person was the young man whom we so much desired to have with us. He told us his name was "Tiah-na-zi." He who accompanied him told us that the Spaniards called him "Cassalan" and the little squaw was an "Up-sah-ro-kee" [Crow Indian], his wife.

We this evening had indubitable proof of the warm friendship of Tiah-na-zi, who, gathering his blanket round him, ascended the most prominent hill and delivered a long harangue in a stentorian voice, the purport of which was to warn all Indians who might be looking round to keep away and not attempt to steal our horses or do us any mischief, as they would run the risk of being shot; that we were Americans and not Texans, and that he, Tiah-na-zi, was our brother.

Our musketoe bars attracted great attention, and by the aid of the indispensable language of signs we soon made them comprehend their use. They were also much amused at our sketches, and immediately recognised one of the nation whom we had met at Bent's Fort, appearing perfectly delighted, laughingly repeating the name "Tah-kai-buhl." Tiah-na-zi was a man of a very happy disposition and amused us, as he sprung around while constructing his rude shelter for the night, by repeating the words "How d'ye do," "Yes," in playful mimicry of the whites. These few words were all that he could remember of the English language, except a few profane oaths—a severe satire on the moral influence exercised by the white people.

September 14th.—We now traveled down the sandy bottom of the creek for the distance of one-fourth of a mile, several times crossing the broad and shallow sheet of water. Just at the junction with the Canadian we flushed a large covey of quails. Our way now lay along the lowlands on the riverside, where the grass grew tall and the sand was deep. We were so much delayed by various difficulties that our whole day's march did not exceed 8 miles. The bluffs on each side were filled with gypsum of snowy whiteness, crumbling easily. At one time the river swept down to the base of a projecting spur of the cliff. We examined the river, hoping to be able to take its bed and travel round this obstacle. To cross over it would be quite a serious undertaking; but nothing is impossible if man will only clap his shoulder to the wheel. All our men were soon at work, and we succeeded in surmounting the obstruction. Our course being momentarily impeded, and our embarrassments increasing, we resolved to hazard an attempt to cross the river. Men were sent into the stream in all directions, the best ford selected, double teams attached to the wagons, which contained the remainder of our provisions and blankets, and, rapidly forcing our way through, for fear lest the wagons might settle in the quicksands, we triumphantly reached the farther side in safety. The river is about half a mile wide, generally shallow, though in some places belly-deep to the mules, and the water deeply tinged with red sedimentary matter.

The riverbanks were everywhere covered with tall cane grass from 6 to 8 feet high, and the gravel from which it sprang was whitened in many places by a gypseous efflorescence. A short distance below our ford we found pretty good camping ground, where we pitched our tents. We noticed large flocks of the green-winged teal [Anas crecca] and the brant, Anas bernicla, and Canada goose, Anas canadensis. The last-named bird is easily domesticated. Its long, slender neck and graceful movements render it a beautiful ornament for the ponds and lakes of pleasure grounds.

Our Indian friend endeavoured to astonish us by describing a six-barrelled pistol which he had seen in the hands of some of the Comanches, and we explained in return the superiority of our percussion-locks, pouring water over them and then firing them. It is surprising how perfectly we can exchange ideas by means of mere gesticulations.

We saw today many rattlesnakes, and to our astonishment we noticed one which never gave the usual warning signal;[32] but on killing it Vachard pulled off the rattle, which silenced all our doubts as to its species. Wild turkeys were very abundant, and our people killed great numbers of them. In the evening, while sitting around our camp, Hatcher discovered a large scorpion. It was of a light brownish yellow color, and resembled the Scorpio europæus.

This is our 31st encampment since leaving Bent's Fort, and we determined its position to be in latitude 35° 47′ 56″, longitude 101° 35′ 47″.

September 15th.—Looking round upon the hilltops this morning, we noticed singular objects which, cutting [?outlined] against the clear sky, appeared large enough for Indians, but on closer scrutiny proved to be a drove of turkeys, which always leave their roosts at early dawn.

12. INDIAN WAYS · MEXICAN TRADERS FROM TAOS WITH A PUEBLO GUIDE

While breakfast was being prepared, we remarked the studious nicety with which our Indian friends performed the mysteries of the toilet. They had carefully treasured a little vermilion; this, with the aid of a comb and looking glass, which we lent them, enabled them to complete all their arrangements satisfactorily. We obtained the sketch of them as they were thus employed, seated around their little fire; for they do not like ours, saying, "The white man builds a fire so large that he cannot go near it."

Continuing on down the Canadian, we found all the country around us composed of gypsum, such as our American farmers use to manure their land, and which they denominate "plaster." Doubtless Providence, in His bountiful goodness, has here placed this mineral, which may be all that is necessary to make the soil extremely fertile. It is often white as the driven snow. Rains which percolate it, being conveyed to the river, impart the singular nauseous taste peculiar to its waters. In some ponds which had been evaporated, we noticed that the bottoms were incrusted with a white efflorescence, which some of our party mistook for salt, but its taste proved this formation due to the gypsum. The bottomlands were very well timbered with cottonwood, which in some places formed extensive groves. In many places we observed the Cucurbita aurantia, loaded with its golden globes. Plum trees are in abundance, and grapevines in wild luxuriance completely enshrouding the shrubbery which upheld them.

Tiah-na-zi, who volunteered his services as scout, reported that he had seen some Comanches and had given them chase. They had doubtless obtained a glimpse of the main party and were not at all disposed to be overtaken. He soon after came to our camp in company with several Spaniards. When he first saw them he had raised the war whoop and started to give them chase, but they, finding themselves pursued by a single individual, awaited his approach. They proved to be a small party of traders, who had come out under the guidance of one of the Pueblo Indians, and told us they had been twenty days in reaching this place from Taos, in New Mexico. They were dressed in conical-crowned sombreros, jackets with the stripes running transversely, large bag breeches extending to the knee, long stockings, and moccasins. They were badly armed, and presented a shabby and poor appearance though we learned that they were a good specimen of the class to

---

32. A rattlesnake does not invariably advertise its presence, though its common device for keeping trespassers away is to vibrate its rattle—the train of horny segments at the end of its tail. It does not act from altruistic motives in "warning folks off the trail"; it just doesn't want to be stepped on. The sound it makes is more nearly a buzz than anything else, and once heard, it is not likely to be forgotten. For all sorts of information on rattlers, and on tall tales told about them, see Laurence M. Klauber, *Rattlesnakes* (2 vols.; Berkeley and Los Angeles, 1956).

which they belong. They are called "Comancheros" and make frequent trading excursions into the country of the Indians with whom they exchange their stock for horses and mules, which the Indians frequently retake before they reach their homes. Their defenceless state gives the Indians little to fear. They suffer them to traverse the country even whilst they are at war with the Mexicans.

We had scarcely selected our camp ground when our young Indian friend ascended a high hill and while sitting there fired his gun, as a signal, as we afterwards learned, to some Kioways who were encamped in the vicinity and who soon came to visit us. One of them recognized us, having formerly seen us at Bent's Fort, where we desired him to tell the Indians we were coming among them. He, thinking it would be a capital joke, reported that a large body of Texans were coming down the river. The Indians had fled in all directions, and he was laughing heartily at the consternation he had created, and said, "I told them a big lie, but now I've told them the truth." They informed us that their best warriors had gone to fight the Mexicans.

13. Farewells · Search for the Washita · A Tarantula · Staked Plain

As this was the point where Hatcher was to leave us, he commenced making preparations to return to Bent's Fort. It was with much regret that we saw him depart. He had, by his gentlemanly deportment, won upon the regard of all, whilst, by his knowledge of the people and country, he had rendered much valuable service in our intercourse with the Indians. Having bid us farewell, he started with a single companion, Mr. Greenwood, to make his way to Bent's Fort. He was well acquainted with the road, and set out in the night, to escape any Indians who might be lurking about our camp.

Here, too, our Kioway friends were to leave us in the morning, and we were quite at a loss what to give them. All that we could gather consisted of a few pieces of tent cloth, tobacco, powder, and lead for the men. Some few individuals deprived even themselves of their knives. These articles were arranged in three piles, so as to present an imposing appearance, and our Indians were called in to receive them. They appeared well satisfied, and said "they were now rich." We afterwards gave them a few needles and some thread, with which they were delighted. They generally use the awl and leather cord or sinew, which is preferred for sewing skins, as the leather does not cut them. This sinew is generally obtained from the "fleece" of the buffalo, where it lies in a broad sheet along the back muscle. It can be divided and subdivided so as to form a thread of any degree of fineness. The Indian, with his blanket, awl, knife, bow and arrow, can house, clothe, feed, and defend himself. In going to war, or in long excursions, they generally carry several pairs of moccasins, finding convenient storage for them between the skins which form their snow-white shields.

September 16th.—Our instructions compelled us here to leave the Canadian and seek the head of the Washita, or, as the Indians call it, Buffalo Creek. Having made all preparations for the start, we bade adieu to our three Indians. Tiah-na-zi had shown himself so devoted to us as to gain the hearts of all, and looked as if he only wanted an invitation in order to accompany us. His eye and whole manner told us that his heart went with us, and with a gesture peculiar to the Indians he signified his deep attachment for us. Last night I was awakened by his deep groaning, and thinking he might be suffering under the influence of the nightmare I went to him and uncovered his face; in a little while he appeared to return to himself, and told me he had been talking with the Great Spirit, and was deeply affected by the concern I had manifested for him, and in the morning touchingly alluded to it again. He reiterated the warnings given us by Hatcher, and the Kioways we saw yesterday, against leaving camp or separating any distance from the caravan when on the march, for the Comanches have been known to charge down and lance a straggler in the sight of his friends, who, being mounted on mules, are unable to overtake them to revenge such an outrage.

They had also told us that Red Jacket, one of the Comanche chiefs, who had been highly enraged with the Texans on account of their late difficulties, had gone with his party to the Antelope Buttes, and that most of the other tribes had exhausted their supply of meat while awaiting the arrival of Bent's wagons and were scattered around in search of buffaloes.

We were to follow the False Washita[33] as far as the "Sand Hills" and then regain the banks of the Canadian, which we are to trace to its junction with the Arkansas. Ascending the bluffs, we bore away in a southeasterly direction, and our wagons rolled along rapidly over the prairies, which for some distance had been swept by the fire; and although the grass had started afresh, there was still a desolate blackness spread around. Here we noticed the tarantula, the legs 2 inches long, which would make the spider over 4 inches across. Some tribes of Indians extract the venom for the purpose of poisoning their arrows. It is said that all injurious effects may be prevented by the application of black mud or by suction.

We moved pleasantly along with but little obstruction until obliged to cross the sandy bed of Arrow Creek, a fine stream of pure water, remarkably straight, and well timbered with characteristic cottonwood, and lined along its banks with excellent pasturage. Stopping here a few moments in order to refresh our horses, we resumed our journey, but soon found ourselves involved in sand hills some of which we noticed on our right of considerable height and marked the head waters of the creek upon which we were to encamp. We reached Elk Creek about 2 o'clock, but by following the directions given us had struck it too high, and there was no water. Beyond, we were sure it was not to be obtained and therefore commenced to descend, looking anxiously along its sandy bed in search of the desired element. After following the sandy route about two miles, we found a sufficient supply, with a fine site for our camp, on a high tongue of land deeply indented with buffalo paths, between the junction of the forks. Here we observed great numbers of the nighthawk, Caprimulgus americanus, which were darting around us in all directions, frequently passing within our reach, while the plover, Charadrius vociferus, along the bed of the stream, was ever and anon sending up his lone melancholy cry of "Kill deer."

September 17th.—This is the day which we shall look back upon in our wanderings as the day of anxiety. After disentangling ourselves from the labyrinth of ravines which form the head of Elk Creek, between whose forks our route lay for the first four miles, we entered upon the famous tableland known to the Spaniards as "El Llano Estacado."[34] This is the most extensive and continuous of the plains lying in the desert country, and gives rise not only to the Washita but to all the main branches of the Red River, as well as the rivers of upper Texas or their affluents. To reach the headwaters of the Washita it was necessary to cross a portion of this dry and level tableau. The only water found on this extensive region is contained in pools or lakes, often at great distances asunder and with banks so low that the traveler, unless familiar with the locality, often passes them unnoticed.

The sun was pouring down heat as heavy clouds do rain; and as it rebounds from the surface of the pools, so did the heat appear to rebound from the extended level of the prairie. These reverberations gave rise to the phenomena commonly termed mirages, so often observed in the desert, where every object appears distorted and generally in motion. The purity of the atmosphere, the looming, as sailors term it, and the numerous ascending currents of heated air, contribute to produce this effect; so that you often see a tuft of grass dancing on the horizon—a tree, or bush—

---

33. The Washita was sometimes called the False Washita to distinguish it from the Ouachita (or Washita) that is further east. It was also called the Río Negro; see Gregg's map. It roughly parallels the Canadian, some ten to twenty miles below that river, until it runs south to the Red, whereas the Canadian continues eastward to the Arkansas.

34. The phrase still awaits a satisfactory explanation. With reference to the high plain in northwestern Texas and southeastern New Mexico, east of the Pecos River, it is usually translated as "Staked Plain."

whilst you are ready to mistake a rabbit bounding across your path for a deer, or perhaps an elk. Herds of buffaloes have been taken for forests of trees, and a buffalo's skull, with a projecting horn, for an Indian prancing about on his white steed.

We traveled some hours in the direction indicated by our friend Tiah-na-zi, but had found no sign of water. Our tongues seemed to cleave to the roofs of our mouths, and our throats were parched with dryness. The rude joke and boisterous laugh had long since died away, and the "Hep!" of the driver as he urged his panting team under the scorching sun grew fainter and fainter until we moved on in dead silence.

The idea of having been misled evidently began to steal into our minds, though not a word was spoken; but the tales we had heard by the campfires, of treachery, surprise, and massacre, were evidently revolving in our minds. This sort of depression, akin to fear, is contagious; and as we pursued our way each one examined his rifle and closed in with the main body. An Indian, mounted, now appeared and, as he swept along the horizon, looked a very giant; another and another burst upon our view, on every side, which led us to believe that we were surrounded. Of their intentions we knew nothing, still less of their numbers. A white flag displayed failed in attracting them to our camp, and they still hung around our flanks, watching our movements. These were moments of fearful forebodings. Could it be possible that the wily savage had laid a plan to decoy us upon this broad desert, rich in the bloody legends of travelers, but to make us an easy prey? Many bore up against this conclusion, while others were by no means so sanguine.

14. On the Washita · Alarm but No Indian Attack · Kioways Friendly

In this state of suspense we traveled for some hours, when we observed some slight irregularities in the horizon. Soon the falling of the ground became evident, bringing back hope to our hearts. A long line of bluffs was now visible, and with elastic rapidity all our forebodings vanished. The camp was completely metamorphosed from gloomy despair to glad delight. Some laughed, some whistled, others sung, and the loud crack of the teamster's whip told more than words could convey. All laughed at their fears, and as we descended into the breaks of the headwaters of the Washita we could have met, fought, and conquered a legion of redskins. The day which had begun in gloom and despair ended in joyful mirth, a fact that shows the contagious nature of both fear and joy, as well as illustrates the sudden changes a man's mind may undergo—passing from one extreme to the other.

We descended by a rough, tortuous path to the channel. In one spot where the sand was damp we noticed recent tracks of a bear and her cubs, as well as of wild turkeys, the latter of which game appeared to be very abundant. Our loose animals, rendered wild by their suffering for water, were running in advance of the party in spite of the efforts of their drivers. After a march of 2 miles, we found a place where the water rose through the sand and where we encamped with the usual precautions.

In the evening we saw Indians on the bluffs, but no sign of amity could induce them to approach our camp. Their skill in following and spying out others, without being themselves discovered, is truly surprising. Mounted on horses, they will hover around a party day after day, and unless some experienced person be of that party, no one else would suspect an enemy near. Their knowledge of the country and their dexterity in detecting your route are such as to enable them always to keep out of your direct path. Throwing themselves on the flank of the column, they preserve any distance they please, approaching under the shelter of a bluff or in the bottoms of ravines, and again receding on the broad prairies. They get the direction of the line of march by throwing themselves in the prolongation of the column, and by signs convey intelligence of any change in your direction to their friends around.

Early in the morning we noticed two buffaloes, and one of our people went in pursuit, but they were too wary to be approached. When the horses are in good order, "running" is the most certain mode of taking them. The hunter then prefers the double-barrelled fowling piece, being short, light, and easily handled, which, with a good horse, insures the game. He is brought close alongside of the buffalo, and the heavy ounce balls make a mortal wound, which, once thrown by a good hunter, never needs to be repeated; but, continuing the chase, he selects a second victim. The high plain over which we passed produced only poor grass and a few cacti. The stream is lined with quite a vigorous growth of vegetation, among which the tall cottonwood stands pre-eminent.

We determined our position to be in latitude 35° 25′ 41″, longitude 101° 05′ 00″.

September 18th.—Warned by the suspicious conduct of the Indians we had seen through the day, we made all in readiness, for we knew there was no hope of quarter, retreat, or succour. Every heart was animated with a firm determination to repulse the foe.

It was scarcely dark when the mules showed signs of restiveness. Once, the cry of "Turn out!" resounded through the camp and all sprang instantly to their feet. We found on inquiry that one of the guard, Walter Harding, had seen several dark figures stealing along close to his post. Balanger pointed out several as they glanced slyly over the ground in passing from bush to bush, but he was directed not to fire unless the Indians endeavoured to enter camp. Thus for a great part of the night we were robbed of our sleep. At length they must have become alarmed at our watchfulness and retired, for our mules, which had stood gazing eagerly into the darkness beyond the chain of sentinels, with their long ears projecting rigidly forwards, now commenced quietly feeding, and we returned again to rest.

This morning we displayed our flag and soon saw our tormentors slowly peeping over a neighboring ridge, while others seemed to burst forth from the ground quite near us. They proved to be Kioways, and had, as we supposed, mistaken us for Texans, and said they had crept near in order to hear us talk and thus be able to decide whether or not we were their enemies or were Americans. Upon being told that we spoke exactly the same language, they appeared quite disconcerted. After shaking us cordially by the hand, they asked to warm themselves, complaining of the shivering cold they had endured last night, as well as of hunger.

We gave them some tobacco, and they kindly offered to guide us on our way as far as their village. Some of the Indians told us that we had the honor of entertaining "To-hah-sun," or Little Mountain, the head chief of the nation. He was a man of middling stature, quite fat, with a very wide mouth, upon which there played a constant smile, and his whole face showed an intriguing character. We found him very intelligent, and he directly comprehended that we required a much smoother route for our wagons than they do for their lodge trails. He said that we were now on Buffalo Creek, and informed us that Cut-nose Creek was nearly at right angles with this stream, and that we could not reach it without suffering much for water. We therefore determined to continue down this stream until opposite its mouth and [to] detach a party for the purpose of making the reconnoissance.

Little Mountain had many inquiries to make in regard to our adventures. We spoke of our having met with Tah-kai-buhl, who appeared to be well known to all the people. He asked about Hatcher, whom he designated by imitating his habit of putting his finger in his eye and pulling down the lower lid—an action of similar import to the gyratory motion of the hand previously mentioned, and which was used by Hatcher when he thought the Indians were endeavouring to get too good a bargain in trading. He said he wanted greatly to see him, and that he loved him very much. Hatcher appeared to be a universal favorite with all the roving tribes that had ever dealt with him.

We now crossed to the left bank of the creek and encamped in a delightful nook shaded by tall cottonwoods and affording plenty of grass, where we stopped to refresh our weary animals and receive the visits of the village, which was near. Old men, squaws, and children soon flocked around us, eagerly offering to trade, and appeared much dissatisfied because we had nothing to exchange with them; for they had expected to obtain some memorial of the coming of the "Tab-bi-boo" or Americans, which to them is a great gala day; and they care little if they pay double the value of an article, provided they have something to show and to say when the village gossip commences.

We now placed before them a map of the country, which had been made out at Bent's Fort by Tah-kai-buhl at the suggestion of Mr. Fitzpatrick. Quite a council was called to decide whether or not Buffalo Creek runs into Red River or into the Goo-al-pa, as represented on the map. A clean sheet of paper was produced and the map drawn according to their directions. But the council being composed of old men, to whom great deference was paid, and a great discrepancy of opinion existing among them, like most celebrated politicians, they at length agreed to compromise, and represented all the rivers as running parallel, ad infinitum. Tah-kai-buhl's map was corrected, and the relative positions of the various topographical features were preserved in a surprisingly exact manner, when we consider that it covers an area of about 800 miles in length.

An old man, the father of Little Mountain, particularly attracted our attention. He was wrinkled and thin, bearing evident marks of extreme old age. He wore on his head a sealskin cap, a very unusual circumstance, as they seldom cover the head. On his shoulder hung a tattered uniform of a Mexican soldier, a triumphant memorial of the daring prowess of his son, to whom he was also indebted for his handsome little Spanish wife. She told us that she had been their prisoner four years and that the Kioways and Comanches had a number of Texan prisoners.

The old man was garrulous and incessantly importuning us for gifts, making numerous inquiries in regard to our nation and our object in venturing upon the prairies. Mr. Simpson informed me that a young chief named The Bear appears about to rival Little Mountain in his authority over his tribe, over whom he will exercise despotic sway. He mentioned an instance in which he caught at his lance and rushed at one of his men for some trifling disobedience, saying he was a chief and determined to be respected as such; that he always moves about in great state, constantly attended by a young man, his aide-de-camp, whose duty it is to attend to all his wishes, spreading a buffalo robe for him to sit upon, lighting his pipe, &c.

We noticed that many of the women had their hair cut close to the head and their faces deeply gashed and covered with clotted blood, in mourning for some departed relatives. They presented a revolting sight, not being allowed to wash the face until the time of sorrowing had elapsed.

Fearing that the company of the Indians might be troublesome, as they appeared much dissatisfied with our inability to trade, we again took up our line of march and proceeded 14 miles down Buffalo Creek, and encamped in a fine bottom. The traveling now became more favorable, and the country, too, looked smilingly, for it was evident that we had passed the great desert; and we hailed with delight the signs of fertility, and now looked forward to the successful eventuation of our expedition. We were told that the Comanches on the Canadian, hearing of our approach, had decamped and betaken themselves to Cut-nose Creek, where they were in a state of great alarm and in considerable numbers. We saw their trails and, from the size, inferred that the accounts we had heard were not exaggerated.

15. FITZPATRICK'S REMARKS ON THE VARIOUS INDIAN TRIBES AND LANGUAGES

As events have led me to say much with reference to the Indians, it may not be amiss to introduce in this place some valuable information which I some time subsequently received from Mr. Fitzpatrick. He says "that there were two great roots from which have sprung all the different tongues spoken by the Indians now and hitherto inhabiting the northern and western portions of the Union, together with all the territory east of the Rocky Mountains, with the exception of a few tribes which have no resemblance of language whatever to the others, and are the Pawnees, Arickirees, Mandans, Cheyennes, and Kiowas; these tribes, I think, have originally belonged to the extreme southern part of the Union, or far in the interior of Mexico.

"In order to inform you better in regard to the two roots spoken of, I will here name some of the tribes belonging to each: The first and most numerous are the Sioux, Kanzas, Osages, Ottoes, Ioways, Mahas, Punkas, Saux and Foxes. And besides these there are numbers of others which have a close affinity to the above-named. The other root is the Iroquois, to which belong the Shawnees, Delawares, Chippeways, Tuscaroras, Mohawks, and, indeed, all the New York and Canadian Indians, together with those bordering on the Lakes, the State of Ohio, and Indiana. But now that they have become so crowded and mixed together on the western and northern frontiers, they are fast losing their originality, and it is even now difficult to classify them. The Crow or Upsarokee Indians live along the eastern base of the Rocky Mountains, and is one of the most formidable and warlike tribes in all that country. Their language is also a dialect of the Sioux, and is very harmonious and agreeable to the ear.

"I will now cross the Rocky Mountains, by the way of the South Pass; and in going over I would like to take with me the Comanches and place them where they properly belong, among the Shoshonee or Snake Indians, as I found their language exactly the same; and with them I would also place Ottowas, Poncas, Sanpitch, Piutas, Timpanutas, together with all the very numerous small tribes in the great desert west of the Salt Lake and lying between the Columbia River on the north and the Colorado on the south, all of which belong to the Shoshonee or Snake nation.

"I next proceed to the north fork of the Columbia, all along which we find numerous tribes altogether differing in character and language from any we have yet met with, and in naming them will begin above and descend the river, thus: The Cotonary, Flathead, Collespillum, or Pond de Neil [Pend d'Oreille], Spogan, Nepzerces, Kiuse, Wallawalla, and many other small tribes, all of which speak a similar language, but so very harsh that few of our people have ever made any progress in attaining it.

"The Chinooks are the remnants of a once powerful tribe near the mouth of the Columbia and more properly belong to the coast Indians, who differ much in language and appearance from those of the interior, and I believe might, with greater propriety, be arranged and placed with the islanders of the Pacific than with any of the inland tribes. The whites have never been able to learn the Chinook language, but they have manufactured a sort of gibberish out of English, French, and Chinook, which all talk and understand.

"In regard to cannibalism, I think it has never been a custom of our northern Indians, or the western tribes, particularly those of the Rocky Mountains. However, the custom of offering human sacrifices prevailed, I believe, amongst many of them in former times, but has gradually ceased, until it has finally been abandoned almost altogether; so much so, that I have only known one instance of a ceremonial sacrifice in the whole of my experience. Nevertheless, I have reason to believe it was once a custom of many tribes; and at the conclusion of the great ceremony which always took place on those occasions, the medicine men and braves of distinction would eat of the victim, more perhaps for the purpose of perfecting the ceremony than for any relish they might have for human flesh.

"Those poor miserable wretches inhabiting the great desert west of the Salt Lake, and who I have before noticed as belonging to the Snake nation, are no doubt cannibals, for they will eat anything whatever, either animal or vegetable, that is not poisonous, and have been known in many instances to devour their own offspring: this occurs from desperate necessity. They are fast decreasing and will in a short time become extinct."

The coup counter

Aug 9th 184[?]

September 19th.—Followed the Indian trail which we struck yesterday and which led along the left bank of Buffalo Creek. The country was sandy, and high ridges ran along on each side parallel with the stream. The traveling was now fine, with the exception of the sand hills which it was necessary occasionally to pass. The country had a more inviting aspect, the streams heavily timbered, with broad valleys, and few bluffs such as we had labored through for so many days. The bottoms of the streams assumed a more luxuriant appearance and became more tangled, while the uplands were thickly spread over by a diminutive species of oak commonly called "shin oak," not exceeding two feet in height. We occasionally saw clumps of oak of greater size. As we passed on we were able to trace the windings of the famous Cut-nose Creek, and found that instead of being the main branch of the Washita it was but an insignificant tributary of a few miles in length. Towards the latter part of the day the river appeared but sparingly scattered with cottonwoods; and the banks becoming higher, we tried the bed of the river, which is now perfectly dry except in the immediate vicinity of the mouths of its affluents, the waters of which are not absorbed so rapidly by night as by day, when the absorption of the heated sand, and the direct evaporation of the atmosphere, occasion a very perceptible diminution. The river's bed is here 200 yards wide; banks low, and covered with driftwood, showing that it is subject to the same phenomenon that we witnessed on the Canadian.

Today we saw several deer ploughing through the deep sand of the river's bed, and the innumerable tracks of the wild turkey showed that they must be very abundant. Our camp ground was covered with the sunflower, [family] Heliantheæ, among which we noticed a variety the flowers of which were sessile and axillary.

We had now effected the main object of our divergence, having obtained three tolerably well determined astronomical points on the headwaters of the Washita River; and, having passed the buttes at which we had been directed to leave the river and return to the Canadian, we resolved to do so on the following day.

September 20th.—As we were not positively certain that we had reached the sand hills, not having seen any which were remarkably conspicuous, although there is quite a ridge of sand buttes on the right-hand bank, we continued to follow the river and became involved in difficult ground, which was high and rough, composed of red clay filled with gypsum, which is found so generally to pervade this country. The waters percolating the immense masses of this mineral separate the sulphuric acid from the lime and acquire an extremely nauseous taste, anything but agreeable to wayworn travelers, although our animals appear to relish it much. The gypsum is often crystallized in the clay banks, where it is beautifully transparent and resembles mica. The water is also unpleasant to wash in, being exceedingly "hard," curdling the soap—which, however, is easily remedied by adding a little wood ashes.

The river, which all this morning appeared to bear northeast, now makes an abrupt bend to the south; we therefore determined to leave it and strike for the Canadian. To the southeast we traced the river by the high ridge of land which loomed up through the haze. Its bed spreads out to the width of 300 or 400 yards and, being composed of deep sands, so absorbs the water that nothing can be discovered but a mass of fine, white, siliceous particles moving in the breeze. Sandy beds, formed by the disintegration of the rocks above, form a characteristic of all the streams in this country; and the rivers that we follow one day, deep and rapid, may the next sink in the sand and disappear. The strong wind heaps the sand upon the banks, forming constantly changing hillocks and often advancing inwards like the dunes on the seacoast. The course of the streams may be traced for miles, on a windy day, by the drifting clouds of sand which hang over their beds.

We now begin to lose trace of the Indians and congratulate ourselves on being nearly through their country.

Today we found plenty of the oak and cottonwood. The bottoms were filled with grapevines and plum trees, and we passed several groves of hackberry; and the plains were varied with a beautiful species of Labiatæ [mint]. We noticed the meadow lark, the shore lark, and several kingbirds, Muscicapa tyrannus—the first we recollected to have seen.

After traveling 14 miles we reached a little bowl-shaped valley surrounded by sand buttes and cottonwoods. The night proved exceedingly chill, and had we not selected this position we should have suffered much from cold. We could not help contrasting our preparations for sleep in this country with those of our comfortable homes. Each one now lies with his gun in hand, the muzzle towards his feet, and knows not that he will ever again see the light of day.

Our latitude is 35° 19′ 57″, and longitude 100° 29′ 53″.

September 21st.—Today we carried our resolution into effect and left Buffalo Creek, bearing a little north of east, passing through a country which presents quite a novel sight—the prairie being on every side dotted with knolls, and these covered with oak, looking like small islands, and possessing an indescribable charm to us, who are easily captivated by anything beautiful, and different from the dead-looking prairie, where grass parched by the long drought had not one trait of the delightful green upon which the eye so loves to rest. In the grove we found great quantities of the pokeweed, Phytolacca decandra, the berries of which afford abundant food for the many varieties of birds frequenting this region, particularly the turtledove, Columba carolinensis, which we saw in great numbers. We noticed, too, a singular flycatcher, Muscicapa milvulus, remarkable for their great agility in darting about, which singular movement is greatly facilitated by its long forked tail. The quail and the prairie chicken, Tetrao cupido, started from beneath our feet.

16. Wild Turkey for Dinner · Grapes · Antelope Buttes · A Panther

After marching 16 miles, we pitched our 38th camp near a large grove of oak trees which had evidently formed the nightly resting place of a large flock of turkeys, the ground being strewed with feathers and in many places marked with their scratchings and tracks. We got a great number of these valuable birds, which was a grateful change in the fare to which we had been accustomed for so many days past.

Our invention was now taxed to mend a broken wagon, which being made without hounds, we could not, as usual, affix the tongue to the axle. After much labor, we succeeded so well that this wagon needed no more repairing during the whole journey.

We were obliged to kill one of our beeves, whose feet were so much worn that it could travel no longer. Contrary to our expectations, it proved to be in good order, and had stood the journey well, having accomplished 560 miles in 33 days. These beeves were much more hardy than those taken out with us, owing to their having been brought up entirely on the prairies.

Some turkey buzzards, Cathartes aura, had taken possession of a grove of dead timber and were quietly making preparations for night when some of our party, mistaking them for wild turkeys, sallied forth with desperate intent. They, however, were so fortunate as to frighten away the birds, which doubtless saved them a disagreeable adventure with these carrion eaters; for, it is said, when wounded, they will sometimes disgorge such torrents of filth as to produce the effect of the most powerful emetic on one who should attempt to capture them. These birds show the wary hunter the remains of butchered buffalo, when, on inspection, he discovers that the animal has come to its death by the bullet of the white man or by the arrow of the Indian and thereby judges of the vicinity of friend or foe. Thus the flight of birds, movements of wild animals, a stick, a stone, or even a bruised reed, speak volumes to the practised eye and have saved many a traveler from a cruel death.

September 22nd.—We bore today a little more towards the north, continuing our way over a country similar to that we saw yesterday. About 10 o'clock we made a halt at a well-timbered creek which, from description, we supposed to be Lone Tree or Big Tree Creek. Here we found delicious grapes, unsurpassed in flavor by any we had yet tasted. After stripping the vines, we carefully searched but could find none equal in quality. After resting a couple of hours and then following a creek bed for a few miles, we crossed a divide and encamped at the head of a stream which we at first thought emptied into the Canadian.

Near us was the site of an old Comanche camp. The remains of wigwams still standing covered several acres of ground and must have been the resort of a multitude of Indians. As we approached, an immense flock of turkeys were frightened from their resting places and scattered over the hillside. On examining the old Indian camp we concluded that they had wintered there. We observed circular holes and singular rings, which always mark the site of the medicine tent. Although the days were excessively warm, the nights were cold and we generally had frost before morning.

Ever since meeting with our first band of buffaloes on the Canadian we have been watching for them in vain until yesterday, when, crossing the divide, we found by the abundance of signs that we were entering upon their range. Deer were plentiful and would frequently bound forth from the thickets which lay in our route.

September 23rd.—We were obliged to make a very zigzag course during our morning's travel, on account of the deep ravines of red clay which are not perceptible to the eye glancing over the surface until one arrives directly upon their brink. For a few hours it appeared impossible to proceed, so entangling were these ravines. The country had become quite rough and broken by buttes of red clay and gypsum, in all the varied forms which we had before noticed. We also saw hills composed of very friable red sandstone. The bottoms of the streams were very well timbered, and among the various trees we noticed the cottonwood, elm, black locust, Robinia pseudo-acacia; black walnut, Juglans nigra; and the coffee-nut tree, Gymnocladus canadensis, which contains, in its large legumes, a very palatable nut, which we collected and ate.

We saw numerous small bands of buffaloes today, and judged, from their wildness and the scarcity of signs, that they had but recently arrived and had been lately run by the Indians. One of the party found an arrow stuck into the ground which could not have been there long as it bore no evidence of exposure to the weather, but we saw no fresh signs of Indians. The night being clear and bright, we obtained observations, which gave for our latitude 35° 37′ 53″, and longitude 99° 41′ 03″.

September 24th.—We rolled rapidly along this morning at the rate of 3 miles an hour, intending to make a long march in order to reach the Canadian. We stopped about two hours to noon on the banks of a stream the broad bottom of which was enriched with a splendid growth of timber, making our hearts glad; for the sight carried them back (as the Indians express it) to the land where the timber grows. We were obliged to cross two deep tributary runs, and their high banks gave us much trouble. Near our camp there was a large band of buffaloes, which our men endeavoured to approach by crawling a long distance through brush and brier, and were about to shoot when someone near, seeing a wild turkey, fired, which raised the buffaloes and thus disappointed them. We were soon again on our route, still bearing strongly for the north.

The stream we have been tracing now bends back upon itself in a southeasterly direction. As it began to grow late, we were several times on the point of making our evening's halt, when at length our perseverance was rewarded by the sight of a long line of sand which filled the air and skirted the horizon, and which, like a cloud of drifting snow, hangs over the dry bed of the river and forms a very good guide for the traveler. About 20 miles to the west of our camp lay the Antelope Buttes. There are five of them, two of which appear perfectly conical, and the group which is figured in the accompanying sketch forms one of the most noted landmarks in the whole country. They lie very near the 100th meridian, and therefore are sometimes called the "boundary buttes."

Whilst we were riding along on the edge of a deep ravine, peeping into it in search of water, a loud shouting burst from the party behind us, and on looking round we saw that a large panther had started from his lair in the jungle near by and was bounding away over the hills. Such an unusual sight produced quite an excitement, but we were so wearied by our long march that we did

ANTELOPE BUTTES IN A BEND OF THE CANADIAN RIVER

not attempt to take him. Here I found a fine covey of quails which had taken refuge in the jungle, and prepared a fowling piece to shoot; succeeded in wounding one, and, while intently searching in the narrow ravine for the lost bird, my eye fortunately rested upon a large rattlesnake coiled in the narrow path. The report of my gun echoed through the ravine, and when the smoke cleared way there lay the scattered fragments of the snake. Shuddering at the danger I had escaped, I soon gave up the search for the quail and returned to camp.

The command appeared in excellent spirits at having regained the bank of the river, for each mile now counts on the homeward route, and the cold nights warned us to hasten on.

The river is here half a mile wide, with a small stream winding through its sandy bed, the water turbid and red, with a nauseous flavor due to the gypsum.

September 25th.—About 7 o'clock, our usual hour for starting, we were joyfully moving down the ravine when we soon struck the river and attempted to travel in the bottomland, but [we] were at length forced into its bed, where the sand, being deep and giving way beneath the wheels of the wagons, made them drag so heavily that we were obliged to ascend the high land above us. The banks, where they had been cut into vertical escarpments by the corroding waters, presented to our view strata of gypsum 2 feet in thickness, preserving the general curvatures of the ground; some were curved and broken, some horizontal. We saw numerous bands of buffaloes but had no good opportunities of killing any of them. The route was extremely rough, continually cut by deep ravines and ridges which made the traveling about as laborious as it was on the sandy bed of the river. On many of the steep ascents our people had to dismount and assist in forcing the wagons up the slopes.

In the evening we again encamped on the side of a deep and narrow ravine. Here Harding, who was an excellent shot with the rifle, killed a fine buffalo bull about a mile from camp. Being the largest we had seen, I went out to make a sketch of him and brought in his scalp, which was covered with hair 13 inches in length. We observed here great numbers of the nighthawk, Caprimulgus americanus, which seemed particularly fond of darting about among our mules and horses. These birds have been common on our whole route, as well as the lark, Alauda cornuta, which we found scattered over the prairie from June until late in October.[35]

We were much disappointed at the progress made today; for, having struck a deep bend of the river, we had made nearly as much northing as easting, which added nothing to our advancement.

September 26th.—Seeing that the river again recurved towards the south, we kept away from its bed to avoid the many little ravines with which its banks are serrated, also to shorten the distance by proceeding straight across the bend. We noticed that the buffaloes were in great commotion today, running about in all directions and on all sides; and, as it was not because they had got the wind of us, we therefore supposed that Indians must be near, but afterwards concluded that they were on a frolick. At one place we found a large flock of prairie chickens, which were so unaccustomed to the effect of firearms that we killed a number before they attempted to fly.

We were greatly assisted through many difficult passes by following the buffalo paths, and found that they always led us out by the choicest routes. These animals being so large, and seemingly averse to great exertions, have been endowed by nature with an instinct which invariably leads them to select the most gentle ascents and descents, enabling them to seize every advantage which the ground offers. These paths are also remarkably straight, and as the animals generally move in file they are deep and remain distinctly visible for a long time.

Shortly before we arrived at our camping ground, we reached a small, level plain, gently sloping towards the river, and for the last three or four miles our wagons rolled along quite merrily. From the tufts of grass which covered it we started great numbers of the meadow lark, Alauda magna, which, sailing a short distance, would light on some little shrub and carol forth its melodious song as if wishing to hold musical converse with our party; but the majority of us were thinking of fat buffalo ribs and gave but little heed to the little songsters. Seeing a fine band of buffaloes remaining under the dark shade of a cottonwood grove, close to the edge of the stream upon which we intended to camp, two of our men were selected and sent forward in the hope of procuring meat. A badly directed shot broke the shoulder of a fine cow which nevertheless escaped their grasp. After camping, some of the men went out and killed a cow and a large calf, but as it was late and the meat some distance from camp we preferred leaving it to batten wolves rather than risk men and mules out of camp after dark.

One of the stars upon which we wished to observe was too high early in the evening; we were therefore obliged to be up as late as half past 11 in order to get our observations of Lyra. We were forced to use the brightest stars, as the cold quickly condensed the moisture upon the glasses of the instrument. We found our position to be in latitude 35° 55′ 00″, longitude 99° 11′ 03″.

Here we noticed the site of an old Comanche camp and, on searching about, found near it a place where water oozes directly from the bottom of a ravine and is there free from the nauseous taste which characterizes that at the mouth of the stream.

September 27th.—This morning we crossed the river in order to keep on the inner side of the bend. We find here quite a change in the appearance of the country, as it is completely covered with a dense growth of oak commonly called black-jack oak. As the trees were not more than 30 feet high their branches did not oppose a very great obstacle to our progress, for we managed to force our way through with but little assistance from the axe. In some of the bottoms, where the trees were of a more luxuriant growth, we found the bur oak, Quercus macrocarpa, and collected many of the

---

35. Since this mention of October is made under a September date, it is to be supposed that Abert completed his statement after his return to Washington.

acorns, for they were new to many of us and the singular beauty of the deeply fringed edge of the cup which enveloped the acorn, and the size of the fruit, could not but call forth our admiration. We saw many bands of buffaloes, many composed entirely of bulls. The sexes are said generally to separate at this season.

Towards the latter part of the day we made a difficult descent and crossed a small stream the banks of which were in many places very high and perpendicular. We saw impressed on its moist sandy bed tracks of bear, deer, and turkeys. Among the smaller birds were the nighthawk, flicker, meadow lark, quail, and turtledove. In the vicinity of our camp we found some old charred logs and well-bleached buffalo bones, showing that Indians had been here some time ago.

The forests of black jack which we had passed through today stretched back from the river as far as the eye could reach, and we took every opportunity to examine [them] from the highest practicable points. They form a portion of the celebrated "Cross Timbers."[36] The right bank, or south side of the river, has been entirely free from timber. This point is frequented by great numbers of deer and turkeys, which at this season obtain an abundant supply of food from the mast, which literally covers the ground. I noticed that some of the mules were very fond of acorns. The buffaloes appear more numerous in our path than on any previous day, although we expected that on entering the timber we should entirely lose sight of them.

Sunday, September 28th.—We had quite pleasant traveling today, as the bottom was smooth and we were fortunate to find no obstacles to our progress. As we saw that the river made a new bend, we crossed it, after a march of 8 miles, to the right-hand bank. The north side still continues heavily timbered, while the side we are now on has not a single tree to enrich the broad uplands. Along the bluffs which skirt the river we still find the never-failing cottonwood. We stopped about 11 o'clock to give our weary animals a little time to rest, as well as to allow them to get a little of the luxuriant grass that grew in a low bottom by the riverside, where we found excellent water which oozed from a marshy spot near our halting ground. Here we noticed rare sounds that were perfectly new to us. On investigating the cause we found they originated from small quails, which certainly spoke a different language from that used by the civilized birds of the same species.

On our route this morning we met an old bull which appeared quite reluctant to move out of our road; at last he took shelter in bushes within a few rods of our line of march. He looked old and was so gaunt that his skin hung upon him like wet drapery upon a skeleton.

Having refreshed ourselves, we again pursue our route on the bed of the river, which in some places, where the sand is covered with red clay, can be traveled upon without difficulty. The sand is very deep, and our animals sink to the fetlock, which renders our progress laborious.

When we had marched 13 miles, we saw at the mouth of a little stream the banks of which were beautifully shaded with cottonwood a drove of wild horses engaged in playful gambols. On perceiving us they stood for a moment, all eyes, gazing at the singular appearance, then circled rapidly round the spot where they had been standing, with their wide nostrils close to the ground, keenly snuffing the grass, and then dashed up the river with their long tails and manes floating in the air. One of the handsomest, a large roan, came boldly up towards the head of the column and galloped slowly along so as to view the whole command, then turned gaily off to join his happy company. We find the buffaloes still very abundant.

Upon looking back to our last evening's camp we saw that the prairies were on fire, and sup-

---

36. Lieut. Wheelock's journal of 1834, p. 91, describes the Cross Timbers as "a timbered thicket, small black-jack saplings so dense as to frequently require the ax to make a road for a horseman." "Forests of cast iron," said Washington Irving in chap. xxi of *A Tour on the Prairie* (1835). On Gregg's map (1844) the wooded strip is an eastward-bending arc, its upper tip above the north fork of the Canadian River, in the Indian Territory, and its lower tip below the Brazos, in Texas.

posed that our own campfires had been the cause, and felt much grieved at this unnecessary destruction of vegetation which a benign Providence had intended for the nourishment of many of His animated creatures.

Our whole march today did not exceed 17 miles.

September 29th.—Very soon after leaving camp we again attempted to travel in the bed of the river, and after proceeding a short distance we found, as usual, that the wagons cut deep in the sand, which obliged the mules to labor heavily. We therefore again resorted to the plain, forcing the wagons up the high bluffs of red clay which form the banks. We traveled along on the right bank of the river for nearly 11 miles, when we crossed to the north side and found ourselves hemmed in on all sides by forests of black-jack oak, diversified with little prairies, which afforded great relief and gave us opportunities of obtaining a wide survey of the country, and at the same time enabled us to select our route. The buffaloes were around us on every side, and the deer and wild turkey find pleasant hiding places by the side of cool streams which are shaded by large timber of almost every variety.

17. FISHES SEEN AND A FEW SMALL ONES CAUGHT WITH A MOSQUITO BAR

After marching 16 miles we encamped at the source of a small creek which in several places along its course widened into small lakes of 5 feet in depth, the transparent waters of which were enlivened with the roach and the sun perch. We caught a few small ones by means of a musketoe bar. The signs of the turkey were very numerous, and on all the streams we crossed tracks of the otter, Lutra canadensis, were observed. We saw two flocks of the green-winged teal and several turtle-doves. Harding killed a fat cow within a short distance of our camp, and we had rare feasting on the marrow-bones and hump ribs.

For the last 3½ miles of our day's journey the bluffs became very high, varying between 200 and 300 feet. The country on this side of the river, as it recedes from its banks, is heavily timbered with several varieties of oak, particularly the black jack.

The night was extremely cold, and the stars bright, and a fine clear sky; we therefore were enabled to get several series of astronomical observations, which gave us a latitude of 35° 51′ 59″, and longitude 98° 45′ 23″.

September 30th.—We were all awake at an early hour, as the coldness of the night forced us to the fireside, when we heard a detailed account of the alarm which occurred last night. It appears that while one of our sentinels, Patrick Bradley, was walking his post, from some unaccountable cause his gun went off. Startled by the report, he for some time thought that the Indians had fired on him, but on examining his rifle and finding the charge and wiping stick gone he began to think that at least he had not been seriously wounded.

No sooner had the grey of daylight begun to spread over the eastern sky than our mules commenced to bray a loud reveille, wishing to be loosed from their pickets that they might glean their scanty morning's meal, as they were then let loose to graze under the protection of the horse guard, who are always ready to drive them into camp in case of an alarm. The lasso is never removed from their necks, which makes it easy to take them when necessary to saddle them previous to prosecuting our daily march. We were obliged to leave one of our horses here as his back had become incurable and was now so very sore, the blowflies having got in, that we could not use it. Many others in our band were suffering greatly from the same cause. Calomel is the only effectual remedy, and we were not so fortunate as to have any of it with us.

After traveling over a country very similar to that which we had passed the last two or three days, we made our halt at 12 o'clock near a small stream where we procured good water and permitted our animals to rest and recruit their exhausted strength. Here we found the skin and bones of a black bear and inferred the presence of Indians. Again on the way, we traveled on slowly, for the day was hot and water had been very scarce.

We at length reached a fine creek with banks high and exceeding steep. Crossing it, we encamped on the top of the hill, which proved very fortunate on Lieut. Peck's account, who might otherwise have been obliged to spend a night in the woods. He says: "I had wandered out with my rifle in search of turkeys, and continued down the ravine towards the river, crossing ravine after ravine till night set in. I now turned to go back, but found the road longer than I expected; still, I trudged on, but a little doubting. After the lapse of an hour I began to think I had lost my way. Ascending a knoll, I saw the light of the campfire two miles distant, and had the pleasure of reaching it before the hour of retiring."

We here shot several green-winged teal and numbers of the wild turkey, and one of the men caught a water-hen [mudhen], Fulica americana, which proved very fine eating.

October 1st.—We were obliged to make a very long march without accomplishing much, for the creeks, with their many branches, forced us to make innumerable detours, which caused us great toil and only delayed our advance. Although we marched only 15 miles, we did not form our camp until it was very late.

After clearing these troublesome ravines, the country became beautiful, covered with "shadowy forests [and] with champains riched, with plenteous rivers and wide-skirted meads."[37] Its surface was gracefully undulating, with long swells, the valley everywhere heavily timbered, and the prairie land covered with a luxuriant growth of grass. Mr. Fitzpatrick appeared enraptured with the scene and said he had not seen such country for more than four years. Bands of buffaloes were feeding on every hillside, and deer and turkeys unusually abundant.

We noticed today, on the opposite side of the river, about 8 miles distant, a long line of high buttes, which we concluded formed the dividing ridge between the Canadian and Buffalo Creek or Washita.

The weather is now becoming very cold and we find the ground every morning covered with frost.

18. Lovely Country · "Glorious Vegetation" and "Glittering Forest"

October 2nd.—The lovely country which we have now entered still continues to spread its glorious vegetation before our eyes, so long accustomed to the barren soil of the great desert. Buffaloes were so abundant that we resolved to procure a good supply, and before the timber was cleared away which shaded the ravine on which we were encamped, we discovered a large band which had almost surrounded our camp. Pierre Balanger and Solomon Rivarre were selected to act as hunters. We made but a short march of 8 miles and encamped on a high bluff bank by the riverside, and waited anxiously for our men, who did not get in until late. They had been so fortunate as to kill five cows. Many of our men who had crossed the river were also successful. We therefore had the greatest abundance of fine fat meat.

The day has been extremely cold, with sharp east wind, and the foliage around gives signs of approaching winter. The leaves of the oak are turning brown; the red sumach contrasts with the yellow grasses, and the glories of the forest trees come rustling at the shaking of the rude blast. Notwithstanding the chilliness of the air I took a bath, and returned to enjoy a fine supper of buffalo meat; "fleeces," briskets, ribs, tongues, udders, marrow bones, &c., were roasting, boiling, and frying over the merry campfires.

October 3rd.—We have a cold drizzling day; the mist hangs heavily over the country, and the

37. Quoted from *King Lear*, I, i, 65–66.

chill of approaching winter benumbs our limbs. We descended from the highlands into the river's bed in order to pass a wide creek which entered the river about half a mile below our camp. We wondered much at the absence of all signs of trails, or campfires, in a country so beautiful, abounding as it does with game, with timber, with water, with, in fact, all the allurements which would induce man to frequent it. We found the bottoms along the riverside filled with buffaloes, which had undoubtedly taken shelter there from the cold winds.

Towards the latter part of the day the drizzling rain ceased, but still a grey wintry sky cast a gloom over the wide-expanded landscape. At 3 o'clock we came near the foot of an isolated bluff of considerable height, which was surrounded by a thick growth of cottonwood, and which was of great service in warding off the keen blast. The river at this point can be crossed without wetting above one's shoe tops. The drizzling still continued intermittingly and forced us to leave our comfortable campfires and seek shelter in our tents, where we managed to keep warm by wrapping up in our blankets.

October 4th.—The weather, still continuing as unpleasant as yesterday, forced us to remain here "deliberating in cool debate" the greater part of the day. During wet weather the abrasion of the mules' collars is greatly increased; their shoulders and backs were already flayed by the continued friction of the harness. We feel inclined to murmur at the dispensations of Providence, Who in merciful goodness gives rain to fit His creatures for our uses. We at length consoled ourselves by thinking that what was so disagreeable to a few might still yield good to many.

Yesterday evening Bowers shot one of the largest bucks we had yet seen. When we first noticed it lying on the ground, deprived of its skin, it was mistaken by some for one of our small oxen. Its extraordinary size and fatness made us only regret that our friends towards the east could not share in our enjoyments.

Towards evening it cleared up and we immediately embraced the opportunity to advance. After a march of 4 miles, in which we headed a creek lying between our camp and the high butte, we found a good grazing ground for our weary animals. The night being clear, we obtained good observations, which placed us in latitude 35° 28' 00", longitude 98° 14' 21".

The timber now makes its appearance on the south side of the river, and begins to disappear on this side.

Sunday, October 5th.—The sun rose clear and bright, and as its rays sparkled in the glittering forest we felt cheered by the prospect of a pleasant day's journey. The general surface of the country continues lowering, and is on this side but slightly timbered, whilst a heavy forest covers the surface on the opposite side of the river.

We saw several bands of buffaloes, containing bulls only, which galloped off quite leisurely as we approached. Their motion whilst galloping differs much from that of any animals which we have hitherto seen. It consists of a series of elastic bouncings; their hind legs are kept well under them, while the forelegs are extended, and this position seems constantly maintained; they appear to move by elasticity alone, independent of any muscular exertions. After a march of 16 miles, observing some bulls grazing quite near camp, I approached them under cover of a ravine, although not unperceived, for one lying down immediately rose up and stood ferociously glaring at me, with his eyes red and inflamed with rage.

I noticed on the backs of some of them the common cow bunting, Emberiza pecoris, sitting quite composedly. Large flocks of these birds have been our fellow travelers throughout the journey, and were quite familiar, lighting on the ground immediately in front of our mules, and sometimes attempting to find perching places on the heads and ears of our animals. They oftentimes amused us by their antics while engaged in catching grasshoppers that were started up from the prairie grass by our caravan. This employment called forth all their activity, and caused them to throw themselves into the most ludicrous attitudes while endeavouring to catch their prey, which in myriads surrounded them on all sides.

The stream upon which we have encamped is covered with large cottonwood, on the branches of which we noticed many flickers, Picus auratus. The banks were very high and steep, and the late wet weather had rendered them slippery and unpleasant. The sky again became clouded over, and our eyes searched in vain over the dull gloomy grey of the heavens for one blue patch on which to found a hope against the threatening storm, which at length broke gently upon us, but with every prospect of a long continuance. We again wrapped ourselves in our blankets and endeavoured to fortify our patience whilst waiting for better times.

October 6th.—Today began as dismally as yesterday concluded, and for a while we were kept quite busy preparing for this unpleasant weather, not knowing how long it might continue. On looking out we saw the finest globules of rain obliquely descending, and our mules, instead of taking advantage of the time to graze, stood with their long ears carelessly drooping, and their tails turned towards the direction of the storm, shivering under the effects of the cold rain.

The backs of many of our animals have become very troublesome; the flies attack the smallest sores and blow them immediately. We tried to destroy them by using a decoction of tobacco.

Mr. Fitzpatrick related a singular custom among the Sioux, which, as it shows the tribute that virtue elicits even among savages, I have thought worthy of notice. When the whole nation is assembled, those of the married women who have kept their vows faithfully step forward and challenge anyone to say anything discreditable to their reputation; and then, taking an arrow, break it in the presence of the multitude.

The gloom of the day has been increased by the ill-boding croakings of a number of ravens, Corvus corax, which appear to have a decided fondness for hovering over our camp. The poet could not well find a more suitable object by the means of which he might increase his representations of the terrible than these birds offer, with their sombre plumage and sinister voice.

October 7th.—Although the day was still cloudy and we had no prospect of being able to proceed far, we made an early start, before the sky showed signs of clearing up. We had some little difficulty in crossing the creek on which we had encamped, the banks being steep and its bed of quicksand. The chill of the morning exercised an enlivening influence upon our beeves, which started off at a rapid rate, lifting their heads and tails in the air, and it was some time before they could be overtaken. Again we saw plenty of buffaloes, and made several ineffectual attempts to obtain some of their meat.

On our left side we noticed a long line of heavy timber about 6 miles distant, which marked the valley of the north fork of the Canadian. After a march of 13 miles, we encamped at the head of a pleasant stream which joined the river at the distance of 1½ miles. Today we saw specimens of the sandhill crane, Grus pratensis of some authors. They are remarkably shy birds. I had afterwards a fine opportunity of examining some of them which I saw near St. Louis, perfectly domesticated.

October 8th.—Immediately after starting this morning, we flushed a great flock of prairie hens, Tetrao cupido. This country doubtless is full of them, but they are birds which it is difficult to get up without a dog, as they easily elude observation by concealing themselves in the tall grass.

We now traveled on a narrow strip of land between the Canadian and its north fork, which stream appears to be the more heavily timbered of the two, for in looking in the direction of the north fork we saw a dense forest of oaks extending as far as the eye could reach. As buffaloes were still invitingly frisking about us, we despatched two of our men to get meat for the camp. After a short time had elapsed, they returned saying that they had seen two Indians to whom they made signs which were answered by the Indians' galloping their horses in small circuits. Seeing the buffaloes around in great commotion, and fearing they might be caught in an ambuscade, they immediately returned to camp. We expected all day that these Indians would visit us, but were disappointed, and should have concluded that our men were mistaken, had we not known them both to be experienced in prairie life.

While riding slowly along a low bottom covered with tall grass we saw seven of the large gray wolf, Canis lupus, which started up quite near us.

After a march of 18 miles we encamped on the head of an affluent of the north fork of the Canadian, about 6 miles from that river. We saw today great numbers of the meadow lark. Soon as the shades of evening fell around, a large hooting owl, Strix virginianus, commenced a hideous serenade in honor of the comers; but his music, like that of many human performers, was more agreeable to himself than to us, and nearly cost him his life, for some of our party went out to find him, but he managed to elude them, and then, as if in revenge, all night long did he utter forth his doleful song.

We saw today great quantities of the sumach, Rhus glabra. This is much used by the Comanches in making their "kinick-kinick" [smoking mixture], which they prepare by wilting the leaves over a moderate fire. The Shawnees and other tribes about Westport use the inner bark of the willow, while the tribes on the border of the Great Lakes use the wintergreen and bark of the maple; in fact, almost every tribe uses a different plant.

October 9th.—It was impossible to avoid the ravines today, as they run entirely across the narrow divide, forming one continuous cleft. On our left the country appears heavily timbered with dense forests of oak. We are now on the divide which separates Chouteau's Creek from the main river—the country gradually rolling. The bottomlands by the sides of the well-timbered streams were enlivened by the sumach, whose leaves, being at this season of a brilliant red, form a beautiful feature in the landscape. Our old friends the cowbirds danced about and turned summersets in the air with unusual vivacity as they snapped up the grasshoppers which flew around them. These birds rendered themselves very useful by destroying the insects which would otherwise have greatly annoyed our animals, upon whose backs we frequently saw the birds engaged in busy scrutiny.

Having made a long march of 21 miles we encamped on the side of a clear stream; among the timber upon its banks we found the oak and the elm. The thick woods which bordered the river were perfectly impenetrable on account of the luxuriant growth of the greenbrier, Smilax rotundifolia. Today we saw the last of the buffaloes, whose place seems now to be supplied by deer. As we approached our camping ground we saw three break from the covert within short intervals of each other.

We find our camp in latitude 35° 06′ 11″, longitude 97° 32′ 03″.

October 10th.—The elm trees around us were in many places ornamented with beautiful clumps of the mistletoe. Upon some of them which we had cut down we noticed that the plant was covered with a profusion of beautiful pearly berries, which, being extremely mucilaginous, prove nutritious food for birds during the colder season of the year, when nearly everything except the grass seeds is generally covered with snow.

We were early on our way, and traveled about 4 miles, when we struck a trail, and a little farther on we entered the tangled bottom of Chouteau's Creek. Soon after crossing it we were cheered by the sight of the ruins of old Fort Holmes.[38] A lofty gatepost was leaning mournfully over the ruins around, borne down by the weight of declining years and the ravages of time. Here we saw fragments of wagons which by their age showed that the place had long been deserted. There was the scarcely distinguishable road, in many places overgrown with weeds and shrubs. Some of our peo-

---

38. Log-built in 1834 by Lieut. T. H. Holmes, 7th Infantry, this military post was not long in use. It became "Old" after a new Fort Holmes was built further up the river. According to Lieut. Wheelock's reckoning, it was 105 miles westerly from Fort Gibson.

ple, in the height of their enthusiasm, mounted the chimney and unfurled the American handkerchief that it might float in the breeze. It was a grateful sight to all once more to meet certain vestiges of the white man.

We soon entered the trail which had been cut by the dragoons, and shortly after struck into the dense forest. Although the trail was a good guide, it was far from being a good wagon road; we were continually obliged to cut away timber which grew in our way, and clear away that which had fallen across our route, and in many places we had to level the ground where the water had washed the road into deep gullies. Thus our progress was frequently impeded. Now and then we would suddenly burst upon little prairies covered with pretty good grass, but they were so distant from water as to be unavailable, and in the bottoms where water was to be found, for some distance on each side there was plenty of timber but no grass. Still, cheered by the hope of better things, we continued to travel until nightfall, without finding a place well suited to our purpose.

We at last encamped in a bottom overgrown with the smilax, the sharp briers of which were a continual source of annoyance. We procured sufficient water for our wants from a few muddy pools we found near, but which scarcely afforded enough to satisfy our thirsty animals.

We saw numbers of deer and turkeys, and also hogs which had found their way to this place, where they had remained for several years unclaimed by anyone and, having become as wild as deer, are considered fair game. We saw today a few rude Indian shelters, the roofs composed of large pieces of bark.

October 11th.—At early dawn we were again on our route in search of water for ourselves and animals. The ground was covered with a heavy frost, and the cold severe. We traveled through dense forests composed of white oak, post oak, and black-jack oak, with here and there a few diminutive specimens of hickory. Sometimes we met occasional openings or glades. Everywhere the marks of autumn were distinctly visible: the grass looked dead and dry; the trees were shaking their summer dressing, touched by the withering frost, to the ground.

After a march of 4 miles we found a place suitable for our purpose, and here noticed various signs of half-civilized Indians marked upon the trees—both pictures and letters, which we concluded were of Cherokee origin. On a large spreading oak, beneath which we breakfasted, I caused the letters "U.S." to be inscribed, with the date. In a short time we were again on our way, when, in crossing one of the streams, we noticed distinct prints of a newly shod horse, which circumstance gave us food for conjecture.

In some of the bottoms we found the persimmon, Diospyros virginiana. The fruit was not quite ripe; therefore but few of those who were acquainted with its peculiar astringency could be induced to taste it. The undergrowth was of a complete entanglement of smilax. We again encamped near muddy pools that scarcely afforded sufficient water for the night. The length of our journey today was 16 miles.

Sunday, October 12th.—When we arose it was yet dark. We marched 6 miles before stopping to breakfast. Our road was firm and gravelly, and near our halting place we found a fine spring. For several days we had been keenly on the lookout for wild hogs, and this morning the alarm was given, when all rushed out, gun in hand; in the tumult, someone cried out that they were marked, but the warning was a little too late, for at the crack of a rifle one of the hogs instantly dropped. We regretted the occurrence, but it was now irremediable; so, as other philosophers would have done, we consoled ourselves by devouring the ill-fated animal. The marked hogs, and the frequent cracking of rifles which we heard around, apprized us of our approach to Indian settlements.

After resuming our march we proceeded about 3 miles and entered a beautiful prairie about 8 miles square. We observed a large party of Indians with their squaws, who, we conjectured, had been to render their homage to the Great Spirit. Amidst the luxuriant growth of grass which

Apache Warrior

clothed this broad champaign, the lowing herds were quietly grazing. With glad hearts we hailed these harbingers of approaching civilization. Far, far away in the distance, and in the direction of our route, we saw huge volumes of smoke rising upwards in heavy columns, which warned us to be in future more careful of our campfires, now that we had reached pasture grounds that might be considered private property. We encamped on a pretty stream near a spring delved by the crystal waters in the solid rock. The forest this morning was alive with crows, Corvus corone, and we readily approached them although we were all armed. Our day's march was 14 miles.

October 13th.—Shortly after starting we left the old road and inclined towards the river. We soon struck an Indian trail that led us over a rugged country. We now were obliged to keep a party in advance, with the axe constantly in hand, widening the road and clearing away the fallen timber. Towards the latter part of the day we reached a high and precipitous bluff which limits the river bottom. Having accomplished this difficult descent, we formed our camp at its base near a pond of water. After filling our buckets, we suffered the horses and mules to drink the rest, leaving us without a drop for our morning's meal. A crackling fire of oak sent forth an untiring flame, which dispelled the chill of a gloomy night.

In the wooded country through which we passed today we noticed many varieties of the oak, Quercus obtusiloba [post oak], **Q.** ferruginea [black jack], and **Q.** alba [white oak]. A few specimens of hickory, the ash, and grapevines seemed to have found a grateful soil, and had entwined their tendrils around the loftiest twigs of the tallest trees. The nipping frost which had scattered the leaves disclosed the fruit hanging in profuse clusters.

The prairie lands were covered with a rich growth of grass which gave fine pasturage for the herds of cattle that the Indians had left to roam unrestrained while themselves were engaged in their annual hunting excursions, more for the peltries they may obtain than the meat, which, indeed, they cannot greatly need.

October 14th.—When we arose, we found the ground whitened by a heavy frost; we were all in lively motion to circulate the blood and to prepare for our journey. Soon on the way, we were still following the Indian trail of yesterday when we suddenly came in sight of a large Indian village "deserted quite" by human occupants. The fields around, once smiling with green corn, show nothing now except a few bare stalks. The narrow streets were filled with rubbish, the fences broken down, while a few cattle which were feeding in the cornfield cast upon us a look as if we were treading on forbidden ground; and some crows, also, which were perched on the neighboring trees, seemed to gaze on our intrusion with a jealous eye. The houses were built by driving large pickets closely together to form the walls of the four sides, and the roofs were thatched with bark. On some hurdles near the houses we found a species of Cucurbitaceæ, the gourds of which bore a great resemblance to an hourglass.

As we remained some time in order to recover several stray mules, whilst examining the environs of the village we found the bois d'arc, Maclura aurantiaca, the fruit of which is sometimes called the "Osage orange." The wood of the tree is admirably suited for ornamental work, being of a beautiful golden or amber color; but it is necessary to varnish it immediately after it is polished. The fruit was about the size of an orange, the exterior roughened like a blackberry. That which we saw was of a light green color. It is said to be yellow and of an agreeable flavor, when fully ripe.

After some time our people returned with the lost mules. The interim was spent by us in hunting squirrels. In reconnoitring our road for tomorrow those who had books to read did read, "to while away the lazy hours of peaceful day."

In the afternoon, Yount brought in a fine and an intelligent-looking Indian who belonged to a small tribe called "Quapaws." He had found him at a village eating sweet potatoes and milk. He told us that some of his people were encamped a few miles below us, and the rest, with the Kickapoos (near whose village we were located), had gone off to their hunting grounds. We asked him how far we should have to go before meeting with white people. He replied that we could start in the morning and reach them before the sun attained its midday height.

Our camp was situated on a small level plain, about half a mile square, where we remarked two singularly parallel paths, which formed the racecourse, and found one of the sticks with which is played the famous game of ball. We gave our Quapaw friend a few pieces of tobacco, well pleased with the information he had communicated, that on the morrow we should see the faces of our own race. Our people had shot some grey squirrels that made a pleasant change in our daily fare, which we felt was quite meager since leaving the range of the buffaloes.

19. Edwards's Settlement · Creek Indians · News of the 4th of July

October 15th.—After a rugged march up and down deep and steep hills, we were often obliged to dig down the walls on each side of the stream and fill in their beds with logs and sods. At 10 o'clock we reached a level piece of woodland and were slowly proceeding when the sweet sound of the chipping axe, echoing through the forest, fell faintly upon our ears. For a while the distance gave an uncertainty to our surmise. We listened again, and were convinced that we had not been deceived; we rapidly approached the spot whence the sound proceeded, but found only some Creek Indians busily engaged in making log houses. Lieut. Peck and I rode over to inquire the route and the distance to white people's stores, but could get no satisfactory information although we found that one of them spoke English.

Proceeding rapidly, we reached a creek bottom, where we found an abundance of the persimmon. Hastily gathering some of the fruit, we crossed the creek and again saw a very comfortable log house, inhabited also by Creek Indians. We were astonished at the politeness of one, who said, "Strangers, if it is not asking you an improper question, may I be permitted to inquire where you are from?" He put the question with extreme delicacy, for he doubtless supposed that we had been robbing Santa Fe traders, or shooting Indians, as there are some people on the borders fond of such amusements. And the costume of the party was such as would likely excite some suspicion; for we were dressed in buckskin trowsers, with fringed seams; shirts of bright red flannel, and calico of all colors; our hair long and wild, our faces sunburnt and unshaven; and, with our rifles flung across the saddle bow, we presented a formidable, not to say ferocious, appearance. The Indians were dressed most tastefully. Handsome shawls were gracefully twisted around their heads. They also wore leggins and moccasins of buckskin, handsome calico shirts, and beautiful pouch, with broad belt ornamented with massive beadwork. These form the general costume of the Creek Indians.

About half a mile further, we reached Edwards's settlement. Here we met a Mr. Thomas Aird, an Indian trader, who made us welcome to everything the place afforded and politely invited us to mess with him as long as we should remain. Old Mr. Edwards, the patriarch of the settlement, generously gave us a cornfield to camp in. This was a grateful treat to our poor animals; and, as we were the first who used the field since the gathering of the corn, we therefore found a superabundant supply of most nutritious grass. We exchanged here some of our powder, lead, and tobacco (which were now only a burden), for corn, sweet potatoes, and sugar. Thus provided with some of the luxuries of life, we enjoyed our suppers with infinite gust.

We mentioned our having seen wild hogs in the neighborhood of Fort Holmes, and the unfortunate act of killing one that was marked. We afterwards learned that, some years previous, Mr. Edwards had sent a white man and two blacks with hogs and turkeys, to traffic with the Indians. The blacks, for some reason, became alarmed and returned to the settlement. The white man was found a few days afterwards among the charred timber of his cabin, having been scalped by the

Indians. Since that time the hogs have been running wild, and are considered fair game by all who pass through that vicinity.

Mr. Edwards possesses a very large farm, which produces the best corn and as fine sweet potatoes as need be desired. The farm is chiefly carried on by Indians, who, when in want, exchange their labor for the articles desired. We here met with a gentleman from Fort Gibson who informed us of the removal of the troops to Texas. We also learned that the Arkansas River was too low to admit of our going from Van Buren to St. Louis; therefore we determined to cross through the State of Missouri, by the way of Springfield.

The Indians here, like all who hang about the frontier posts, are a trifling set of vagabonds, possessed of all the vices of the whites and Indians without the redeeming qualities of either.

Edwards's settlement is situated on the west bank of Little River, a mile and a half from the Canadian, and, like all backwoods settlements, presents little else than a rude collection of log huts. It is situated in latitude 35° 00' 35", longitude 96° 31' 56". Little River is a fine-sized stream; at the crossing it was 190 feet wide, with a rocky bottom; the banks are about 60 feet high, and the current is quite sluggish; the country around is generally level, soil very good, and plentifully supplied with good timber.

October 16th.—Lieut. Peck and I were up early this morning and started forth with our guns, essaying to kill some of the mallard and brant which are found on the waters of this region, but were unsuccessful. We were greatly annoyed last night by the swine which got into our camp and seized some of the mules' collars that were temptingly greased with the fat of the flayed shoulders of the wearers. These pests oblige us to mount guard as carefully as if we were still in a hostile country.

Mr. Edwards assured us that a few days of good pasturage for our mules would not, in the end, cause us delay; yet, notwithstanding his kind entreaties, and those of many of the settlers, to remain, we were obliged to refuse them, being extremely anxious to proceed; and, at an early hour, bade farewell to our friends and were soon rolling along with cheerfulness and rapidity over a fine wagon road. We noticed many Indian houses with gardens and orchards of peach trees. The country was heavily timbered and rolling. In one place we remarked traces of the devastation made by one of those terrible hurricanes of frequent occurrence in the western world. The noblest trees of the forest had fallen from their high estate and now lay mouldering upon the ground. The contorted piles of wood, the wildly confused directions in which the timber lay, showed the amazing force of the whirling winds.

We nooned at a small run 12 miles from Little River. Lieut. Peck and I then hastened on in the advance of the party to make arrangements with Mr. Stewart, the Creek blacksmith, for procuring corn for our mules and meat for the men. He complained much of the flies, which attack his animals and often destroy them. He mentioned that "Micanope," a Seminole chief, had lately suffered much pain from the same cause, the flies having gotten into his nostrils whilst he was sleeping in the sun, and it was some days before he discovered the origin of his torment. The Seminoles are located on the opposite side of the river, and the agency is between this place and Edwards's settlement. They are now becoming satisfied with their removal, though they must find a wide difference between this region and the Floridas, where everything needful grows spontaneously.

Today we passed through the fire of the prairies while it was burning on each side of the road, without entertaining the least apprehension of danger. This was the fire which we noticed last Sunday, and which must then have been more distant than at present, the wind being now from the east.

October 17th.—Having managed to make an exchange with Mr. Stewart of one of our oxen for corn and pork, we killed the last of our Rocky Mountain beeves, which was still fat and in excellent order although he had traveled nearly 1000 miles. The preparation delayed us until 9 o'clock, when we shook hands with the Creek blacksmith, with many wishes for his success. He had given us several newspapers, among which was a copy of the "National Intelligencer" containing news of the 4th of July.

The prairie on all sides was in a blaze, and the lurid smoke entirely veiled the distant portions of our landscape. Whilst speaking of the little danger to be apprehended from these fires, Yount remarked that in the State of Missouri, and on the frontier where the grass is tall, they are extremely dangerous if the wind be high. The fire then dashes forward with bursting bounds, leaving the grass behind, to the distance of 40 to 80 feet, in the state of live coals, and often progressing with such celerity as to overtake the wild deer. The grass that we now saw on fire was not more than a foot in height. The sheet of flame advanced slowly and steadily, and what it passed over was entirely consumed. Anyone might without risk have stepped through the flame. After we had passed the advancing fires, the prairie appeared as if covered with black crape and as if nature mourned the loss of so much vegetable creation.

The prairie chicken was very abundant, and we also met with large flocks of the little quail; but the most astonishing sight which had greeted our eyes for a long while was three white men, who were dressed in scarlet leggins, with immense scarlet scarfs about their necks. They were certainly laboring under some strange hallucination. We rejoiced to see them free in this wild country where there were no lunatic asylums.

We encamped about 19 miles from the blacksmith's; the country was quite rough, particularly towards the latter part of the march, the prairie land predominating.

We met several negroes on the road who were dressed in the picturesque costume of the Creek Indians,[39] which certainly becomes them well. They are said to acquire the different Indian languages with great facility.

October 18th.—The country today, like that which we passed over yesterday, consisted of level prairies and timberland, generally rolling and stony. After a march of 26 miles we crossed the north fork of the Canadian and encamped at a point about 2½ miles from its mouth. We forded the river without difficulty and found it from 1 to 2 feet in depth; the banks from 40 to 50 feet high and overgrown with large timber, among which the buttonwood stood conspicuous. All the waters of the plain lying between the Canadian and the Arkansas flow into this river, by the way of its two principal forks, which all around here agree do unite about 5 miles above this place.

On the western side of the river we found a flourishing village, and the country around well settled, chiefly by Indians, who cultivate small patches of corn. We succeeded in getting an old cornfield to encamp in and procured corn and fodder from an Indian who resided near us. This man had many questions to ask with reference to the dangers we had passed, and appeared horrified at the wild Indians, as he called them, eating their meat raw. He gave us a piece of bread made of corn meal, and sweet potatoes, which we found exceedingly agreeable.

We saw great numbers of blacks wearing shawl-turbans, which seem well suited to their pseudo-Moorish character. These people are supposed to be superior in intelligence to the Indians, who mostly have recourse to them in their intercourse with the whites. Early this morning we passed a couple of wagons accompanied by three or four men, and afterwards learned that they contained large amounts of specie which the Indian agent who accompanied them was conveying across the country to make his payments.

---

39. See the journal entry for October 15, above. The Creeks, says Hodge's *Handbook*, Vol. I, p. 364, "were more than usually devoted to decoration and ornament." For details of their costumery, colorful and theatric, see Irving's *Western Journals*, ed. McDermott, pp. 42, 43.

Indian Prisoner   Sepr 18^t 1845

A short time previous to crossing the river, Lieut. Peck overtook us. He had been on an excursion to "Tuck-a-bach-ee," one of the principal settlements of the Creeks. He told me that the old chief entertained him well and asked him many questions in reference to his Great Father [the President], and spoke of a visit he had made in company with his interpreter, "Davy Barnett."

Lieut. Peck. describes the occurrences of the day in the following words: "Striking into the woods, I traveled five miles, when I came to a house, but saw no roads except horse paths, and these crossing each other in every possible direction. For 10 miles I now followed these blind guides, passing houses and farms, apparently strewed broadcast over the country, and with momentary expectation of coming upon the town. The sun had well-nigh attained the meridian height when a store was discovered which marked the centre of the town. I was invited by the chief, a fine-looking old man, to go to his house and tell him of my adventures, which invitation I accepted. He spread before me two halves of a watermelon, upon which I began to eat and relate the tale of my journey through the medium of an interpreter. Having finished my repast and tale, I bade the old man adieu and, having a good road, joined the main party at the crossing of the north fork, well pleased with my adventure."

We determined our position to be in latitude 35° 18' 16", longitude 95° 42' 45".

20. SEARCH FOR RIVER'S MOUTH · EXPLORERS OR DESPERADOES?

Sunday, October 19th.—As it was desirable to save our mules as much as possible, Lieut. Peck and I started, with Balanger, to go down to the mouth of the Canadian for the purpose of obtaining astronomical observations, which would enable us to fix the point of the junction of the Goo-al-pa with the Arkansas—leaving Mr. Fitzpatrick with the party to proceed direct to Fort Gibson.[40] Wishing to avoid the regular route and to pursue a more direct one, we struck boldly into the woods, where, after wandering some time, we found the road. We soon saw a house by the roadside, and there were informed that the route had been lately traveled by wagons, so that we would not be likely to mistake the way.

Having reached the crossing of a creek where it was evident that no wagon had passed, or could pass, we concluded to take a middle course, leaving the river on our right hand and the road on the left, when, striking into an Indian trail, we pushed rapidly forward and at length reached a precipitous bluff which seemed to bar all further progress. One of us now ascended a tall tree, that we might get some idea of the surrounding country. It was very irregular, with many high ridges and deep valleys intervening between us and the long misty line which marked the valley of the Arkansas. On our right, high hills entirely intercepted our view of the Canadian. As nothing could be gained by turning back, we determined to persevere, and, all of us dismounting, forced the mules down the precipitous declivity.

After a long march through misty lowlands, where sycamore trees seemed to arch the heavens and gaudy paroquets were circling round with rapid flight and screaming loudly among their lofty branches, we forced our way through the tangled undergrowth of spicewood and smilax and at length reached the banks of the Canadian just as the last rays of the sun were disappearing. Continuing our way through a confused labyrinth of cattle paths and Indian trails, we struck one which led us to a house, the inmates of which informed us that we were 8 miles from the road and 18 from our point of destination. About dark we reached an Indian's house where we procured a

---

40. Fort Gibson, on the left bank of the Neosho River some two or three miles above the confluence of that stream with the Arkansas, served as an important link in frontier defense and communications from 1824 until it was abandoned in 1857.

guide, in consideration of remunerating him well and giving him a mule to ride. Hurrying on, we reached "Webber's Falls," as the desired point is termed, about 11½ o'clock.

We first went to the store to inquire there for lodgings, when we were directed to retrace our steps to Mr. Riely's, a Cherokee Indian, who met us, with gun in hand; but as soon as our voices were distinctly heard, he received us with the greatest kindness. He told us that he had seen us when we first passed, silently moving along, and noticed the glistening of our gun barrels by the rays of the new-risen moon and suspected us to be the "Starr boys,"[41] by which name he designated four notorious outlaws, and had despatched two of his negroes to warn some persons who lived beyond him of our approach.

We immediately commenced taking the necessary observations, but were scarcely ready before the sky was completely overcast, destroying all our hopes for that night. We had traveled more than 45 miles on our mules that had been in hard service since the 12th of June. Having been 13 hours in the saddle, we were well prepared to do justice to the supper which our host had set before us; after which, spreading our blankets on the floor before the blaze of a roaring fire, we were soon asleep, losing all remembrance of the day's difficulties.

October 20th.—This morning we hastily aroused Balanger and sent him to inform Mr. Fitzpatrick that we intended to remain here until we could obtain a satisfactory series of observations, and to desire him to move rapidly on to Fort Gibson, and there await our arrival; for if the night should be clear, we should, in the morning, be on our way to the fort. On looking round the room in which we were quartered, we noticed newspapers pasted up to keep out the wind, among which was the "Cherokee Advocate," containing a proclamation of John Ross,[42] chief of the Cherokee nation, offering $1000 for the apprehension of two persons named Starr, and $500 for two other persons, who were included under the general appellation of the "Starr boys." The reward was for anyone who should take them, either dead or alive. Being all young men, and just the number of our last night's party,[43] we were not surprised at being mistaken for them.

In the afternoon Lieut. Peck and I went out to view the environs of Webber's Falls. We found the country around flat and sandy, but the fine large timber shows a good subsoil. We learned that the sand had been spread over the bottom by the inundating freshets of the Arkansas.

The paroquets, Psittacus carolinensis, were very abundant, and numerous flocks of them were constantly darting round, describing large circles through the topmost branches of the tall trees. We had taken a gun with the intention of killing some of them, which were rapidly sweeping around our heads and uttering screams as if in highest irritation at our bold intrusion within the precincts of their domain with such murderous intent. Their principal food consists of the cocklebur, which they easily dissect by means of their strong bill. Mr. Riely tells me that their flesh is very pleasant to the taste and is frequently sought for by the inhabitants of the neighborhood. We found some of the fruit of the pawpaw, Anona triloba, and black walnuts. We noticed among the sylva the elm and various species of the oak and hickory, among the latter the bitternut hickory, Juglans aurata [Carya sulcata]—a proof in itself of the inundations which have thrown the sand over the bottoms, as it always grows best in a country subject to be overflowed. We also found the buttonwood and spicewood.

41. A band of desperadoes including, notably, Tom Starr, son of a James Starr who came west in 1833. Most of the band were killed in a gun battle with a posse of Cherokees in 1848. See *Niles' Register* for November 8, 1848; also U.S. Cong. Docs., Vol. 474 (1846), 29th Cong., 1st Sess., Senate Ex. Dec. 298, "Message of the President . . . relative to the internal feuds among the Cherokees," esp. pp. 158 ff.

42. Ross was the son of an immigrant from Scotland by a wife only partly Indian. See Hodge, *Handbook*, Vol. II, pp. 396–397.

43. Abert has named three, but not a fourth.

The way from Fort Gibson was literally lined with the wagons of emigrants to Texas, and from this time until we arrived at St. Louis we continued daily to see hundreds of them.

[October 25th and 26th, no entries.]

On the 27th we reached Maysville, where Lieut. Peck left us in order to go round by the way of Westport to take charge of some baggage belonging to the party which had been left there on setting out. Our route across the States of Arkansas and Missouri afforded but little food for comment; it was too well known to give value to observations such as a rapid journey would admit.

We passed through Maysville and Bentonville, in the State of Arkansas, and Springfield, Waynesville, and Manchester, in the State of Missouri.

On the evening of the 12th of November we arrived safely at St. Louis. The next morning the men were paid and discharged and the public property in my care was turned over to Mr. Robert Campbell, the government agent, with directions that it be sold at public auction.

On the 27th of November we had the honor to report to the chief of the bureau on our arrival at Washington City.

Very respectfully, sir, your obt. servt,

J. W. Abert, *Lt. Top. Eng^rs*

To Colonel J. J. Abert,
        Chief, Corps Top^l Engineers.

At night we obtained several series of observations, which gave us a latitude of 35° 28′ 18″, longitude 94° 58′ 11″.

The exact mouth of the Canadian is 4 miles below, but it cannot be approached on account of canebrakes. The river has sometimes been navigated as far as the mouth of the north fork by boats drawing 2½ feet of water, but is, in general, only navigable for flatboats.

21. End of the Survey · Fort Gibson · Overland Journey to St. Louis

We now considered our labor nearly over. So far as the survey was concerned, our duties ceased; but it was necessary to connect our work with some well-known point. We therefore determined to continue our reconnoissance as far as Fort Gibson, where we should take our last observations.

Having learned, upon inquiry, that all the fords of the Arkansas were dangerous on account of quicksands, we determined to ascend the river as far as the ferry opposite the fort, where we could cross without any risk.

October 21st.—Having bid adieu to our Cherokee host, at an early hour we were wending our way along the western bank of the Arkansas. About 12 o'clock we stopped to noon at a house by the wayside. The good man complained bitterly that his best land, by the riverside, had for three successive years been swept of its golden harvest by the inundations, which also carried away his fences. He had, however, a great many herds of cattle, the rapid increase of which, and that attended by small expense, amply repaid him for all his losses. He told me that the cattle winter themselves without difficulty upon the wild grass of the prairie, and as they sell for $5 a head it may readily be imagined that they cost very little trouble.

Like all travelers in a perfectly new country, where the woodlands shut out the view, and where bridle paths are worn into ruts, seemingly on purpose to entangle you, we met with our share of difficulties. But that evening we had the extreme pleasure of laughing at our cares, seated within the hospitable walls of Fort Gibson. Those who have undergone similar privations can appreciate the glad feelings we enjoyed in again meeting with gentlemen and ladies, and participating with them [in] those comforts and elegancies from which we had been so long banished.

We found here several companies of infantry and one of the 1st Regiment of U.S. Dragoons. This post was under the command of Lieut. Col. R. B. Mason of the 1st Dragoons. It would be presumption in me to speak of so accomplished and well known an officer, but I cannot refrain from expressing my grateful sense of the kindness and hospitality with which we were received and treated by himself and his amiable lady, and, indeed, by all the officers and ladies attached to the command.

October 22nd.—This morning the command in charge of Mr. Fitzpatrick arrived and were encamped alongside of the fort. Through the kindness of the commanding officer, who offered us everything we could need, we obtained $500 in specie and provisions sufficient to last the party 25 days. We here took the observations we had promised ourselves, and found Fort Gibson in latitude 35° 48′ 04″, longitude 95° 09′ 00″.

The 23rd proved a rainy day, which we took advantage of by having our wagons, that were much racked to pieces, sufficiently repaired to last throughout the remainder of the journey.

Friday, October 24th.—We were obliged almost rudely to tear our hands from the cordial grasp of our kind friends. The day was beautiful and everything except its name indicated a fine journey. The sky was clear, with a balmy breeze from the south. The raindrops of the preceding night sparkled in the rays of the morning sun. Three or four officers accompanied us about 3 miles, to the summit of a hill, whence we had a fine view of the surrounding country. After admiring the scene for a moment, we again pursued our route, which was now on a good road.

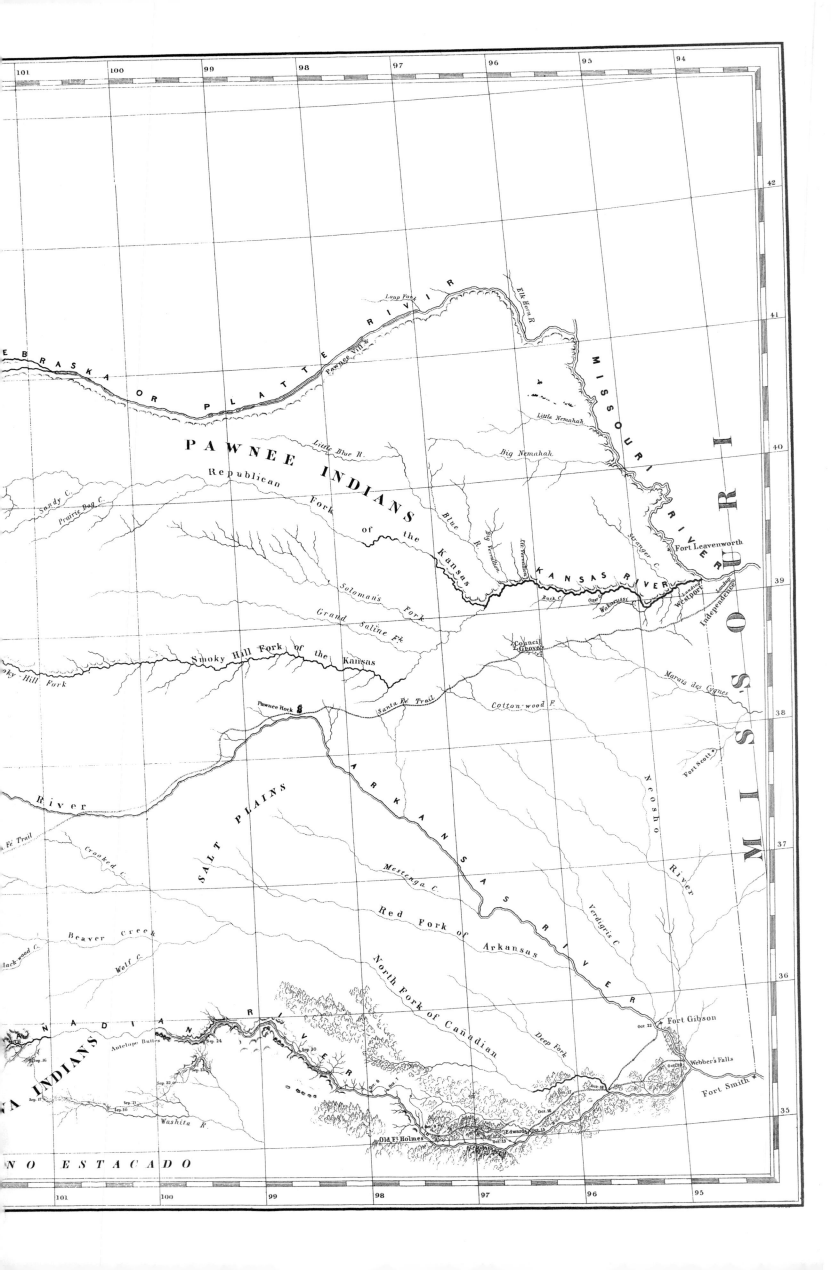

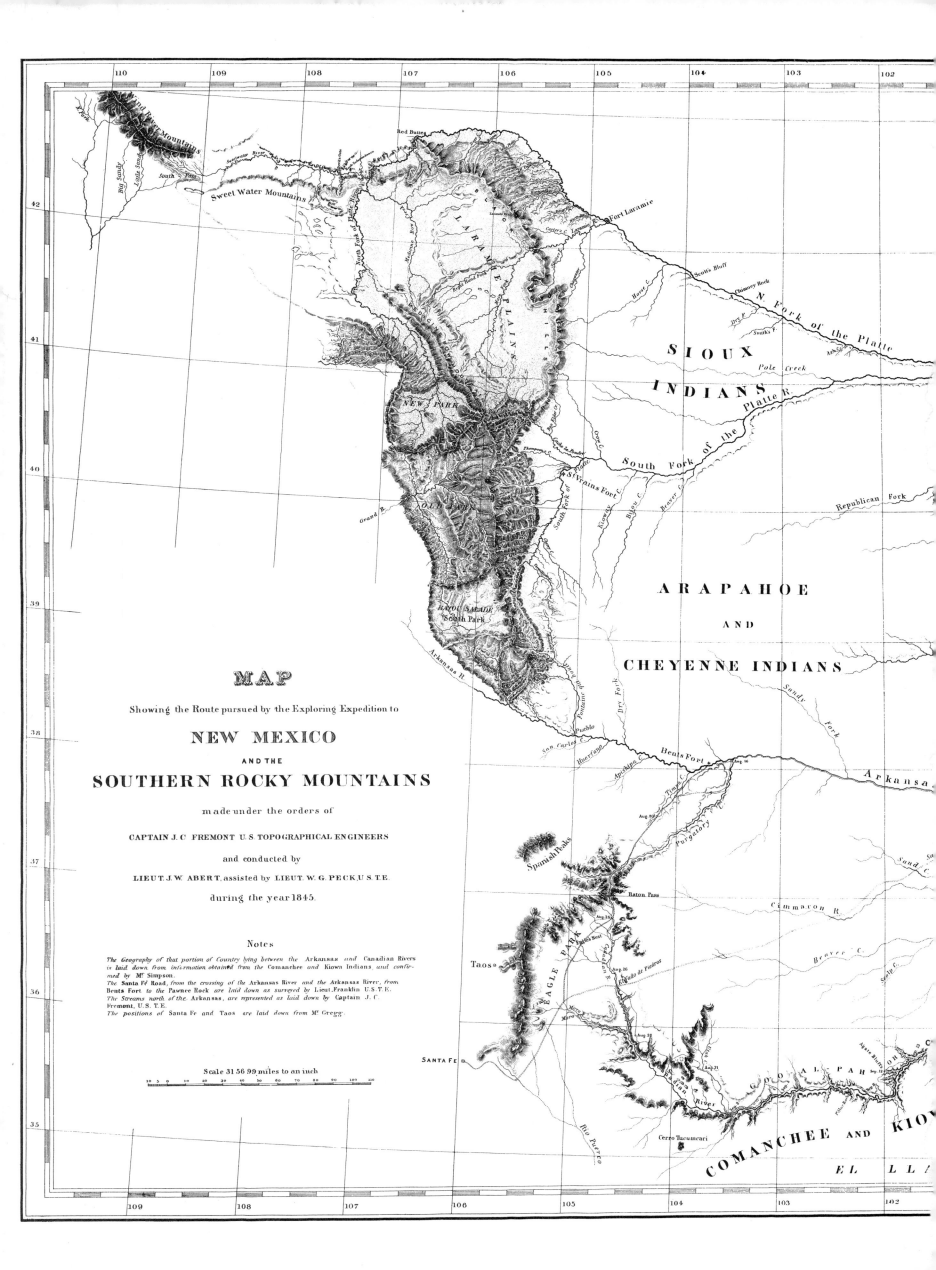

MAP

Showing the Route pursued by the Exploring Expedition to

NEW MEXICO

AND THE

SOUTHERN ROCKY MOUNTAINS

made under the orders of

CAPTAIN J. C. FREMONT U.S TOPOGRAPHICAL ENGINEERS

and conducted by

LIEUT. J. W. ABERT, assisted by LIEUT. W. G. PECK, U.S.T.E.

during the year 1845.

Notes

The Geography of that portion of Country lying between the Arkansas and Canadian Rivers
is laid down from information obtained from the Comanchee and Kiowa Indians, and confir-
med by Mr Simpson.
The Santa Fé Road, from the crossing of the Arkansas River and the Arkansas River, from
Bents Fort to the Pawnee Rock are laid down as surveyed by Lieut. Franklin U.S.T.E.
The Streams north of the Arkansas, are represented as laid down by Captain J. C.
Fremont, U.S.T.E.
The positions of Santa Fe and Taos are laid down from Mr Gregg.

Scale 31 56 99 miles to an inch

GLOSSARY

adobes: sun-baked mud bricks.

angosturas: narrows of a river.

animas: souls, departed spirits.

arroyo: watercourse, wet or dry.

atole: gruel made from Indian corn.

banquette: walk or standing-place for soldiers along the inside of a protective wall.

cache: conceal by burying in the ground.

carreta: Mexican two-wheeled cart.

cibolero: buffalo hunter.

colorado: red.

comanchero: Mexican trader with the Comanche Indians.

duff: sailors' flour pudding boiled in a bag.

enceinte: enclosing border of a fort.

enfiladed: raked by gunfire from beyond one end of a line of protective works or of soldiers.

felloes, or fellies: curved pieces of wood that form the rim of a wheel and are supported by the
   spokes.

gust: relish, enjoyment.

hounds: bracing-pieces that strengthen the underframe of a wagon.

howitzer: short, light fieldpiece, firing a 12-lb. ball. In Emory's "Notes of a Military Reconnoissance" (1848), U.S. Cong. Docs., Vol. 505, 30th Cong., 1st Sess., Senate Ex. Doc. 7, p. 66,
   howitzers of 1846 are described as "small, mounted on wheels ten feet in circumference, which
   stand about three feet apart, and with the assistance of men on foot, are able to go in almost any
   place a mule can go."

kraal: protective enclosure formed by a wagon train. Kraal and corral are related words.

laryetto: lassoer, man skillful with the lariat.

manifesto: list of trade goods, to show to customs officials.

mast: nuts collectively, as beech mast, oak mast, etc.

mesquite: spiny shrub common in the Southwest.

negro: dark in color, not necessarily black.

noon: to stop at midday for rest and refreshment.

palmilla: soap plant, *Yucca alata* or *angustifolia*.

parflèche: rawhide stripped of hair and dried.

pinole: parched Indian corn ground and mixed with water for a drink; "some of the wilder tribes,"
   says Gregg, "use the bean of the mezquite tree instead of corn."

placer: deposit of gold-bearing ore workable by sluicing.

segaritos: cigarettes.

tab-bi-boo: white men; a Shosonean word, variously spelled (tabba-bone, tabba-boo, tabby-boo,
   tab-ba-bo), that appears in the accounts of western expeditions including those of Lewis and
   Clark, 1804–1806, Long, Bell, and Say, 1819–1820, and Frémont, 1843.

tableau: natural scene engaging the interest of the viewer.

taking sketches: making sketches.

tongue: pole of a wagon, to which the draught animals are attached.

vicinage: vicinity.

REFERENCES

Abert, James W. "Journal of Lieut. J. W. Abert, from Bent's Fort to St. Louis, in 1845," U.S. Congressional Documents, Vol. 477, 29th Cong., 1st Sess., Senate Ex. Doc. 438, pp. 1–75, map (Washington, D.C., 1846).

A Government clerk's fair copy, preserved in the U.S. National Archives, is referred to in this book as "the Archives manuscript" of the Journal.

———— "Notes of Lieutenant J. W. Abert," U.S. Cong. Docs., Vol. 505, 30th Cong., 1st Sess., Senate Ex. Doc. 7, App. No. 6, pp. 386–414 (Washington, D.C., 1848).

———— "Report of Lieut. J. W. Abert of His Examination of New Mexico in the Years 1846–'47," U.S. Cong. Docs., Vol. 506, 30th Cong., 1st Sess., Senate Ex. Doc. 22, pp. 1–130, map (Washington, D.C., 1848).

Abert's holograph diary upon which he based this Report has been published under the title *Western America in 1846–1847*, ed. John Galvin (San Francisco, 1966).

An "Extract from the Journal of Lieut. James W. Abert, U.S. Topographical Engineers," which repeats in condensed form the latter part of the diary, is in the letter-books of the Topographical Bureau preserved in the National Archives. It is a manuscript of thirty numbered pages and an unnumbered leaf, undated but marked "Rec'd May 1847."

Bancroft, Hubert H. *History of the North Mexican States and Texas* (2 vols.; San Francisco, 1889).

Boone, Nathan. *See* Pelzer, below.

Dodge, Henry. *See* Kingsbury, and Wheelock, below.

Dunbar, William. "Journal of a Voyage" [on the Mississippi, Red, Black, and Washita rivers in 1804–1805], *Documents Relating to the Purchase and Exploration of Louisiana* (Boston, 1904).

Ellsworth, Henry L. *Washington Irving on the Prairie* [Ellsworth's travel diary of 1832], ed. Stanley T. Williams and Barbara D. Simison (New York, 1937).

Fitzpatrick, Thomas. *See* Leonard, below.

Frémont, John C. *Memoirs of My Life* (Chicago and New York, 1887).

———— "Report of the Exploring Expedition to the Rocky Mountains in the Year 1842, and to Oregon and North California in the Years 1843–'44," U.S. Cong. Docs., Vol. 461, 28th Cong., 2nd Sess., Senate Ex. Doc. 174 (Washington, D.C., 1845).

Repeated in Vol. 467, House Doc. 166.

Also published separately.

Garrard, Lewis R. *Wah-To-Yah, and the Taos Trail* (Cincinnati, 1850).

Gregg, Josiah. *Commerce of the Prairies, or The Journal of a Santa Fé Trader* (2 vols.; New York and London, 1844).

Grinnell, George B. "Bent's Old Fort and Its Builders," *Collections* of the Kansas State Historical Society, Vol. XV (1923), pp. 28–91.

Hafen, Le Roy R., and W. J. Ghent, *Broken Hand: The Life Story of Thomas Fitzpatrick* (Denver, 1931).

Haley, J. Evetts, "The Comanchero Trade," *Southwestern Historical Quarterly*, Vol. XXXVIII (1935), pp. 157–176.

Heitman, Francis B. *Historical Register . . . of the United States Army* (2 vols.; Washington, D.C., 1903).

Hitchcock, Ethan Allen. *The Journal of . . .* (1841–1842), ed. Grant Foreman, under the title *A Traveler in Indian Territory* (Cedar Rapids, Iowa, 1930).

Hodge, Frederick W. *Handbook of American Indians North of Mexico,* Bureau of American Ethnology, Bulletin No. 30 (2 vols.; Washington, D.C., 1907).

Irving, Washington. *A Tour on the Prairie* (Philadelphia, 1845).

———— *The Western Journals of Washington Irving,* ed. John F. McDermott (Norman, Okla., 1944).

James, Thomas. *Three Years among the Indians and Mexicans* (St. Louis, 1846).

Kearny, Stephen W. "Report of a Summer Campaign into the Rocky Mountains &c in 1845," U.S. Cong. Docs., Vol. 470, 29th Cong., 1st Sess., Senate Ex. Doc. 1, pp. 210–213 (Washington, D.C., 1846).
  Repeated in Vol. 480, House Doc. 2.

Kendall, George W. *Narrative of the Texan Santa Fé Expedition* (New York, 1844).

Kingsbury, Gaines B. "Journal of the March of a Detachment of Dragoons, under the Command of Colonel Dodge, during the Summer of 1835," U.S. Cong. Docs., Vol. 281, 24th Cong., 1st Sess., Senate Ex. Doc. 209, pp. 1–38, with map "Showing the lands assigned to emigrant Indians west of Arkansas and Missouri" (Washington, D.C., 1836).
  Repeated in Vol. 289, House Doc. 181.

Latrobe, Charles J. *The Rambler in North America* (2 vols.; London, 1835).

Leonard, Zenas. *Narrative of the Adventures of Zenas Leonard* (Clearfield, Penna., 1839).
  Includes Thomas Fitzpatrick's account of his adventure among hostile Indians.

Long, Stephen H. *Account of an Expedition . . . to the Rocky Mountains . . . in the Years 1819 and '20,* compiled from the notes of Major Long, Mr. T. Say, and others, by Edwin James (3 vols.; Philadelphia, 1823).

Margry, Pierre, ed., "Voyage des frères Mallet" [in 1739–1740], *Découvertes et établissements des Français dans . . . l'Amérique septentrionale* (6 vols.; Paris, 1879–1888), Vol. VI, chap. xii, esp. pp. 455–462.

Murray, Charles A. *Travels in North America* (2 vols.; London, 1839).

Nuttall, Thomas. *A Journal of Travels into the Arkansas Territory . . . 1819* (Phliadelphia, 1821).

Pelzer, Louis. *Marches of the Dragoons in the Mississippi Valley between the Years 1833 and 1850* (Iowa City, Ia., 1917).
  Includes Capt. Nathan Boone's report and journal of his reconnaissance from Fort Gibson in 1843.

Richardson, Rupert N. *The Comanche Barrier to South Plains Settlement* (Glendale, Calif., 1933).

Wheat, Carl. I. *Mapping the Transmississippi West* (5 vols. in 6; San Francisco, 1959), esp. Vols. II and III.

Wheelock, Thompson B. "Journal of the Campaign of the Regiment of Dragoons for the Summer of 1834," U.S. Cong. Docs., Vol. 266, 23rd Cong., 2nd Sess., Senate Ex. Doc. 1, pp. 73–93 (Washington, D.C., 1834).
  Repeated in Vol. 271, House Doc. 2.

Wislizenus, Adolphus. "Memoir of a Tour to Northern Mexico," U.S. Cong. Docs., Vol. 511, 30th Cong., 1st Sess., Senate Misc. Doc. 26, pp. 1–86, appendices pp. 87–141 (Washington, D.C., 1848).

SCIENTIFIC WORKS TO WHICH ABERT REFERS

Audubon, John James. *Birds of America* (7 vols.; New York and Philadelphia, 1840–1844), Vols. II and IV.
     Originally published in London, 4 vols. plates and 1 vol. text, 1827–1838.

——— *Ornithological Biography* (5 vols.; Edinburgh and Philadelphia, 1831–1839), Vols. IV and V.

Bernardin de Saint-Pierre, Henri, *Studies of Nature*, in *Works* (4 vols.; London, 1807), Vol. III.

Cuvier, Georges. *The Animal Kingdom* (16 vols.; London, 1827–1835), Vol. IV.

——— *Cuvier's Animal Kingdom* (London, 1840).

Harlan, Richard. *Fauna Americana* (Philadelphia, 1825).

——— *Medical and Physical Researches* (Philadelphia, 1835).

Murray, Hugh. *The Encyclopædia of Geography*, rev. ed. (3 vols.; Philadelphia, 1840), Vol. III.

Pennant, Thomas. *History of Quadrupeds*, 3rd ed. (2 vols.; London, 1793), Vol. II.

Wilson, Alexander. *Wilson's American Ornithology* (Boston, 1840).

Both Lieut. James W. Abert and his father, Col. John James Abert, were honored in the natural sciences, a finch being named for one and a squirrel for the other.

For "Abert's finch, or towhee," see appendix on birds by Spencer F. Baird in Howard Stansbury, *Exploration and Survey of the Valley of the Great Salt Lake of Utah* (Philadelphia, 1852), esp. pp. 325–326, *Pipilo aberti*: "We have dedicated this species to its accomplished discoverer, Lieutenant James W. Abert."

For "the Abert squirrel," *Sciurus aberti*, Woodhouse, see Spencer F. Baird, *Mammals of North America* ("General Report of the Mammals of the Several Pacific Rail Road Routes," Washington, D.C., 1857), esp. pp. 267–268: "It was first described by Dr. Woodhouse as *S. dorsalis*, but finding the name preoccupied by J. E. Gray for a species from Caracas, he changed it to the one it so worthily bears, for the enlightened and liberal head of the Topographical Bureau, Colonel John James Abert."

Col. Abert was a founder, with Poinsett and others, of the National Institution for the Promotion of Science, established at Washington, D.C., in 1840, which died on the vine. Its collections and library were turned over to the Smithsonian Institution in 1862.

INDEX